THE PARENT COACH

A New Approach to Parenting in Today's Society

Steven Richfield, Psy.D.
with Carol Borchert

D1410092

Barbie is a registered trademark of Mattel, Inc.
LEGO is a registered trademark of Interlego A.G.

ISBN 1-57035-430-8

Edited by Mitchell Duval
Text layout and design by Scott Harmon
Cover design by Scott Harmon

06 05 04 03 02   6 5 4 3 2

Printed in the United States of America

Published and Distributed by

SOPRIS
WEST

4093 Specialty Place • Longmont, Colorado 80504-5400
(303) 651-2829 • www.sopriswest.com

172COACH/9-02/UGI/377

Dedication

This book is dedicated with love and devotion to my wife and colleague, Caryn, and to our two wonderful sons, Jeremy and Jesse. Thanks to the countless children, parents, and teachers who have provided inspiration and input to the development of Parent Coaching Cards over the past several years. It is because of your struggles and triumphs that this tool exists.

— Steven Richfield

This book is dedicated with love to my wonderful husband, Kevin, and to our two beautiful children, Alex and Anna, with whom we share the truest joys of life.

— Carol Borchert

About the Authors

Dr. Steven Richfield is a child psychologist whose work, for nearly two decades, has been focused on child development, parent education, and the emotional problems of childhood. He received his doctorate in Clinical Psychology from Hahnemann University in 1986 and his undergraduate degree in Psychology/Political Science from George Washington University in 1981. Dr. Richfield, a parent with two sons, used his on-the-job training as a parent and extensive clinical experience to develop a new parent training model, one that asks parents to switch from "parent cop" to "Parent Coach." His resulting Parent Coaching program has received extensive national and international attention. Dr. Richfield lives in Plymouth Meeting, Pennsylvania, where he shares an independent private practice with his wife, Caryn. They are the parents of sons Jeremy and Jesse, both of whom provided much of the inspiration for the Parent Coaching Cards.

Carol Borchert received her bachelor's degree in technical journalism from Colorado State University and has been working as a reporter, magazine writer, and author covering a variety of scientific and general interest fields including biomedical sciences, applied human sciences, human-animal bond in veterinary medicine, and parenting. As the mother of two young children, she brings her own experiences to bear in *The Parent Coach* from the front lines of parenting. Carol also works extensively with groups of elementary-age children through volunteer opportunities including teaching, coaching, and community service. Carol lives in Fort Collins, Colorado, with her husband Kevin and their two children, Alex and Anna.

Contents

Foreword

Each year, I offer workshops for thousands of parents. In addition, during my career as a psychologist I have worked with many parents in my clinical practice. These activities, together with the very important experience of having helped raise two sons, have provided me with firsthand knowledge of the questions, challenges, joys, frustrations, satisfactions, and anxieties that are a natural part of the parenting process.

Interestingly, one professional in a well-publicized book advanced the view several years ago that parental influence on a child's development was overestimated. Instead, a child's inborn temperament and peer group were touted as having a more profound impact on the child's functioning than that of parents. While temperament and peer interactions are important factors, I, as well as most clinicians and researchers, believe strongly that these factors lag significantly behind the day-to-day influence of a parent.

It has often been said that while parenting is one of the most important and difficult jobs we face, it is one for which we receive little, if any, preparation or formal training. It is not surprising that as parents engage in the process of raising children, as they seek to nurture qualities such as self-esteem, self-discipline, motivation, social skills, responsibility, compassion, cooperation, hope, and resilience in their children, they search for information and material that will help them.

The quest for knowledge about parenting is evident by a visit to any bookstore. Parenting books fill the shelves. Sometimes the recommendations of one parenting expert seem at odds with that offered by another, adding to the confusion of parents. While all of us may yearn for a book filled with simple recipes, most realize that the challenges of parenting do not lend themselves to set formulas, to a one-size-fits-all approach. Instead, we must recognize the complexity of parenting without allowing this complexity to overwhelm us. Parenting material should serve as a vehicle to transport us from a reactive to a proactive position in which we feel more knowledgeable, comfortable, and confident.

A proactive position goes far beyond a prescription of what to do once a difficult situation arises. Instead, to be proactive implies that parents anticipate challenging moments in a child's development, and they prepare their children to meet those moments with greater assurance and success. This preparation is characterized by teaching children skills and values that they can apply in their daily lives. Ideally, proactive parenting takes place in a calm atmosphere in which children will be most likely to benefit from their interactions with us. In contrast, a reactive approach is often in response to a difficult or crisis situation, a time when neither parent nor child is in the best state of mind to communicate or listen to each other.

While parents can identify many of the issues they wish to address in their child's development, they may feel at a loss of how best to do so. One father recently said, "Every time I try to start a conversation with my six-year-old son and nine-year-old daughter, I'm not certain how to do it. I feel after a minute they have already tuned me out." A mother reported, "My ten-year-old daughter is somewhat shy and hesitant. When I encourage her to try things, she gets angry with me and accuses me of not liking her and trying to rule her life. All I'm trying to do is help her be more outgoing, but, obviously, I'm making matters worse."

I have heard similar comments from countless parents, all of whom desire to be more effective in their parenting roles. *The Parent Coach* by psychologist Dr. Steven Richfield, together with the innovative Parent Coaching Cards that he developed, will serve as an invaluable resource for parents of children of all ages and all temperamental and learning styles. Dr. Richfield introduces the notion of parents serving as "life coaches" with their children, substituting punishment and retribution with teaching and learning. A major focus of the coaching endeavor is to develop effective ways of coping by nurturing our children's emotional and social skills.

As Dr. Richfield so eloquently notes, "Parent Coaches help their children anticipate problems, avoid hazardous situations, and develop and practice the skills necessary to meet and beat challenges. Parent Coaches approach parenting with a high degree of warmth, elevated expectations, and respect for their child's autonomy, but also with firmness and tenacity."

In a truly masterful manner, Dr. Richfield has articulated the major issues confronting children and developed cards that serve as a catalyst to assist parents in discussing these issues in a nonthreatening, nonjudgmental way. He has provided parents and children with wonderful material and metaphors for helping youngsters to remember and apply what they have learned. Phrases such as "thinking side", "reacting side", "cantaloupe skin", "quit the clowning!", "don't take the bait!", and many others will become a natural part of the family's lexicon, influencing parent-child relationships and the lessons that our children learn from us.

In addition to the very rich information and material that Dr. Richfield provides, what is evident on every page of *The Parent Coach* is his empathy for both children and parents and his perceptive understanding of the many challenges they face. To create such an impressive, realistic program suggests that he has drawn heavily from his vast clinical experiences, as well as his own role as a father. Also, his description of the ways in which the Parent Coaching Cards can be applied in the classroom setting underscores his appreciation of the need for parents and teachers to collaborate.

Dr. Richfield is to be complimented for offering parents such a creative, informative, and helpful approach as they engage in the process of nurturing the emotional and social development of their children. His book will be read and reread, and his Coaching Cards will be used again and again by parents. His work will enrich the lives of all families who are fortunate enough to read and apply his ideas.

Robert B. Brooks, Ph.D.
Faculty, Harvard Medical School
Author, *The Self-Esteem Teacher*
Coauthor, *Raising Resilient Children*

Preface

When I began the journey called parenting in 1989, I knew that many lessons awaited me. My parents faced an endless succession of tests and trials raising a family of four rambunctious boys with strong temperaments. The future psychologist in me critiqued the parenting decisions handed down, only to hear the refrain, "Children don't come with instructions." Although I dismissed these words at the time, they sank in deeper than I could imagine. These childhood experiences carved out an intense interest in parenting and an enduring need to develop some instructions.

Carrying that forward, I have been affected deeply by so many people in various walks of life who have touched me through their words and actions, offering support and conviction that children need practical self-control tools to contend with the challenges in our world. While this list is not exhaustive I do want to make special mention of Dr. Bob Brooks, Dr. Russell Barkley, Richard Lavoie, Dr. Harvey Parker, Dr. Myrna Shure, Dr. Barbara Ingersoll, Dr. Tony Attwood, Dr. Clare Jones, Dr. Saul Troen, Carol Gray, Thom Hartmann, Meredith Gould, Andrea Bilbow, Michael Schweitzer, Denise Yearian, Jack Canfield and Mark Victor Hansen, Connie Langland, Theresa DiGeronimo, Julie DeVillers, and Jeff Herman.

On a more personal note, several people stand out as members of the "coaching team," without which the Parent Coaching Cards would never have made it off the drawing board. Marvin Melnikoff and my late father-in-law, Dick Packel, are the most prominent. Natalie Packel, Joe and Ruth Richfield, Bernie and Marsha Richfield, Sue and Neil Sukonik, and Paula and Cliff Goldstein also deserve my heartfelt appreciation. I'd also like to thank the many families who contributed their personal stories to make this book even more meaningful to its readers.

Steven Richfield
March 2002

Chapter 1
WHAT IS A PARENT COACH?

"Here, all mankind is equal—rich and poor alike, they love their children."
Euripides, *Andromache* (c. 426 B.C.)

Introduction

Today's loving parents, much like those of Euripides' time, face many challenges as they anticipate the life journey they will make with their children. While the challenges may be different—disease was the greatest threat to children in the fifth century B.C.—parents throughout the ages have sought to guide their offspring through childhood with love and compassion and to help them become successful adults.

The difficulty for today's parents, of course, is that the world is a much more permissive, fast-paced, and complicated place than it was 2,500 years ago. Our children face a barrage of adverse forces. Social land mines await them at school, on the playground, among friends and peers, on the sports field, and at home. Many children do not possess the skills necessary to navigate these minefields. Disappointments, competition, provocations, inequities, temptations, distractions, and many other pressures can easily jeopardize school-aged children's efforts to keep their lives in balance. Do the following situations sound familiar?

- Your daughter is behaving like a typical teenager, and she isn't even nine years old yet. She's moody and mean to her siblings. She talks back and tells you to not do anything to embarrass her.

- Your son gets in trouble for clowning around at school. He interrupts the teacher, often falls out of his chair, disrupts other kids by talking to them at inappropriate times, and has difficulty staying on task.

- Your son loves soccer, loves playing soccer, and loves when his team wins. But everything changes when his team is losing. He may yell at the other players, get frustrated and angry on the playing field, or cry when the game is over.

- Your daughter has difficulty talking with adults. She can be reduced to tears simply by the thought of going to a restaurant and giving her order to a waitress. Her social awkwardness has you making excuses and talking for her.

- Your son loves to play with other kids but often scares them off because he becomes too bossy and intense.

- Your daughter suffers a complete and total meltdown and is irrational and unreasonable for hours if things don't quite work out the way they were planned—if, for instance, a movie is sold out.

Kids try to find their way through these sorts of difficulties with varying degrees of success and failure. Parents, meanwhile, try to fulfill the many different roles necessary to help their children through such vagaries of childhood. Parenting requires the negotiating skills of a hostage mediator, the organizational skills of an executive secretary, the tutorial skills of an army of teachers, the listening skills of a psychologist, the problem-solving skills of a Nobel physicist, the financial skills of a corporate chief financial officer, the cleaning skills of Heloise, the cooking skills of Wolfgang

Puck, and so much more. Yet, today's parents often are not equipped to help their children develop the "coping with life skills" they need to succeed. Kids without these life skills often suffer from academic underachievement, social problems, damaged self-esteem, missed opportunities, and strained family relationships.

"If only kids came with an instruction manual," many a parent has quipped, only half-jokingly. Unfortunately, they don't, so how can parents help their children develop the self-control and social skills they need to successfully move through childhood and into the adult world? *The Parent Coach* and the Parent Coaching Cards introduce parents to the concept of parent as coach, on the same team with their child, and working together to help their child build the social tool kit needed to succeed.

Trying a New Approach—the Parent Coach

Children's lives are filled with many "decision points" that challenge their social judgment, self-control, and problem-solving abilities. It's easy for them to fall short in any of these skill areas, setting the stage for trouble now, as well as down the road. Most parents deal with such trouble in a reactive mode, focusing on punishment, discipline, and retribution. The Parent Coach approach is to help children develop coping skills in a proactive way that allows them to better deal with the demanding circumstances of everyday life and to prepare for the many challenges that lie ahead. Rather than waiting for problems to occur and then focusing on the fallout, Parent Coaches help their children anticipate problems, avoid hazardous situations, and develop and practice the skills necessary to meet and beat challenges. Parent Coaches approach parenting with a high degree of warmth, elevated expectations, and respect for their child's autonomy, but also with firmness and tenacity. The Parent Coaching Cards at the end of this book reflect the Parent Coach philosophy put in a practical, accessible format for easy and fun use with children. While these cards and this book focus primarily on children ages 6 through 12, parents can easily adjust the messages and delivery for younger and older children.

What Does a Parent Coach Do?

The Parent Coach discusses and practices with his or her child the skills necessary to successfully cope with problem situations. To strengthen children's sense of trust and security, parents must let them know they are on their side and that they will help them figure out why things go wrong, not just punish them for misbehaviors. The Parent Coach style of parenting emphasizes the importance of a safe and nonjudgmental dialogue between parent and child. The child must feel accepted and understood, not criticized and lectured. To do this, the parent has to resist stepping into the role of disciplinarian, as this often causes the child to put up a defensive wall and tune out the parent. Finding the right coaching voice is as important as finding the right coaching style. Many parents overlook this key ingredient in communicating with their children. Children can be profoundly sensitive to a parent's tone of voice and volume. It's not unusual for parents to say the right things but to deliver the mesage with a tone of animosity. It's very easy to lapse into a punishing and blaming tone, which simply works against the nurturing but firm style the Parent Coach needs to have in order to effectively communicate with the child. Finding your voice involves both speaking from the heart and listening with a rational mind.

The Parent Coach focuses on the present as well as the future. While the parent may be in a real-time situation, such as dealing with a child refusing to do homework or a child using bad language to lash out at a sibling, he or she should use the opportunity as a chance to develop the child's inventory of emotional and social skills. Much like an athletic coach keeps an eye on each player's performance, the Parent Coach watches the child to determine where coaching is needed; it may involve helping the child stay tuned in to conversations with friends, respect adults when they are on the telephone, or handle hurtful words from classmates with humor and dignity.

The Parent Coach uses words and body language to show the child that parent and child are on the same side. The old "I'm going to teach my child a lesson" is replaced with the new "What lesson can both of us learn?" This mutual learning is a very important part of Parent Coaching. The Parent Coach accepts the fact that he or she has much to learn as well. Children are far more receptive to a parent's attempts to coach life skills if they don't feel talked down to and if they sense that their parents are in this thing with them. Parents can further this feeling of being a team by sharing with their children stories from their own lives and how they solved problems or how they could have done things differently. Parents can use an "instant replay" of a difficult situation involving their child to look at what went wrong, what went right, and how the child could approach a similar situation in the future.

Social and Emotional Skills

The main goal of the Parent Coach is to develop and refine the child's coping skills. These skills can be placed under two general categories: social and emotional. Social skills include cooperation, sharing, judgment, perspective-taking, taking turns, manners, situation evaluation, conversational comfort, and others. Emotional skills include resilience, frustration tolerance, self-control, perseverance, generosity, and many more. Children are best helped in developing these skills by preparation and discussion, practice, and coaching by the caring adults in their lives.

Each child is unique in how he or she approaches and reacts to the world, but parents usually know their child's "trigger points" (often with greater awareness than the child) and when their child is about to be challenged. Trigger points are situations, events, people, or even words that can set off a child's "reacting side." Identifying common trigger points is a good place to start with Parent Coaching; other skills can be woven in from there. Some common "Triggers to Trouble" are listed below. If possible, you can discuss these triggers with your child or identify other triggers that commonly develop into problems.

CHECK OFF YOUR TRIGGERS TO TROUBLE

❑ Finding out that I won't be able to do something I have really been looking forward to.

❑ Seeing other kids having fun doing something that is against the rules.

❑ Feeling annoyed by the behavior of another kid.

❑ Not wanting to do something I have to do.

❑ Losing at a game or not performing as well at something as I think I should.

❑ Feeling jealous about something involving another kid.

❑ Not being able to accept the mistakes of others.

❑ Feeling very bossed around by someone else.

❑ Finding out that someone used something of mine without my permission.

❑ Feeling pushed aside by a friend.

❑ Having to switch gears from doing something fun to doing something serious.

❑ Not getting something that I want.

Triggers to Trouble often occur because a child's reacting side takes over from their "thinking side." Parent Coaching mainly involves helping children develop the skills they need to keep their thinking side in control, so that they can react to situations rationally and with deliberation. For instance, Trish, mother of eight-year-old Shelby, frequently uses the **When Words Pop Out, Watch Out!** card. Reading and discussing the card with her mom helped Shelby to better understand how wrong words won't help her get what she wants but can often lead to an undesirable outcome, like a time-out.

Getting Started in Parent Coaching

This book and the Parent Coaching Cards in the back can be used in many different ways. Ideally, the parent should read the book to get a good handle on the Parent Coaching approach and the content of the cards. However, many parents are eager to get going with practical tools that can have immediate effects on the behavior of their children. It may help to read this chapter and the "Thinking Side and Reacting Side" chapter before moving on to the cards that you are keen to use.

Notice, too, that most chapters contain real-life examples from families who have used the Parent Coaching Cards since their introduction in 1998. You'll also find lots of examples of "Chalk Talk," where parents play out scenes with their children ahead of time. A Chalk Talk is similar to what a sports coach does before a game, drawing plays on the board and showing players where they need to be and what they need to be doing. Parent Chalk Talks help your child think about situations and how they might be handled. Chalk Talks give your child an opportunity to practice with you before facing the real thing, and they also let you give your child practical input about different tactics, words, and strategies to handle especially challenging situations.

The Parent Coaching Cards are practical, portable, emotional intelligence tools that can help children address hot topics that are affecting them in the moment. Older children may wish to read the cards on their own and then discuss the ideas with you. For a younger child, you may want to read the cards with the child, discussing and clarifying the cards' messages and action words.

The Parent Coaching Cards in the back can be removed and put on a ring to keep them together. The text found on the cards is also included in each corresponding chapter. Your child may wish to color in the drawings on the cards—that's a good place to get him or her interested in a discussion.

You may want to start with a card that addresses one of your child's main trigger points or just with a card that piques your child's interest.

The Parent Coach and the Parent Coaching Cards will help you prepare your child for the day-to-day challenges of growing up by stocking his or her life tool kit with the social and emotional skills that are necessary for a happy, successful life.

PARENT COACHING TERMINOLOGY

Parent Coach: A parent who combines consistent emotional support with a belief in the child's capacity for growth, who has a clear sense of which skills will best help the child cope, and who exhibits reasonable control over his or her own unhelpful reactions.

Parent Coaching Cards: Social and emotional skills cards that help kids deal with the pressures at home, school, and in other social situations so they don't get trapped into behaving badly and suffering the consequences.

Thinking Side: The part of a child's mind that allows observation of himself or herself in social situations and development of appropriate actions and responses. The thinking side helps kids avoid getting trapped by circumstance.

Reacting Side: The part of a child's mind that responds impulsively to the world around him or her, sometimes appropriately and sometimes with undesirable consequences. The reacting side is like a magnet for tough times because it reacts to "traps."

Chalk Talk: The conversation a parent will have with a child to practice different social scenarios or to replay an event that has already occurred to help the child understand and improve his or her ability to respond appropriately to similar situations in the future.

Power Talk: Words and phrases children can use to build their self-esteem so that they can better handle situations or individuals who seemingly have power over them.

Traps: Situations in a child's life that typically trigger the reacting side.

Chapter 2
THINKING SIDE
AND REACTING SIDE

Our brains help us think about the things we do every day—like how to do homework, when to ask for something, and other stuff like that. This **"thinking side" is what "thinks" us through problems and helps us learn how to succeed at life.**

There's also a part that reacts to the world around us—like when we shriek with excitement on a roller coaster ride or yell with anger if things don't go our way. This **"reacting side"** lets us have many kinds of feelings, good as well as bad.

Usually, our **thinking side** and **reacting side** work together just fine. But sometimes our **reacting side** grabs control over our **thinking side.** When this happens, anger, stubbornness, jealousy, and other funky feelings can cause us to say and do stuff that creates all sorts of hassles. This is why it's much better to let your **thinking side** stay in charge and to keep your **reacting side** under control.

These cards will help you do this by teaching you how to think your way through problems you may face at home, school, and with friends. First, each card will teach you about when to use it. Then, it will suggest a **talk-to-yourself message** that you can read or have someone read to you. As you read these messages, try repeating them in your own mind so your **thinking side** can learn them.

Developing the Thinking Side

Children come into this world as reacting beings, not thinking ones. They are basically one big ball of impulsivity. Their senses are the avenues they use to take in sounds, smells, and tactile sensations. They react instinctively to feelings of comfort and pain, hot and cold, and hunger and fullness. Their reacting sides dictates most of their responses to the environment around them. Early in life, our children operate on a stimulus-response level, with no intellect mediating the equation. This early, preverbal developmental stage provides the building blocks of communication. As it unfolds, language begins to fill the mediation-of-thought role between stimulus and response.

Parents play the most important part in developing this mediation between stimulus and response. Parents repeat phrases, give conditioned responses of their own, and lay tracks for the notion of cause and effect. In time, certain behaviors become associated with certain outcomes. The stove is hot = stay away from the stove. The cat bites = don't pull the cat's hair.

As children grow, their contact with the outside world increases, and they learn from these experiences, as well. The thinking process becomes more solid as three and four year olds tell themselves, "Don't do that." These early experiences act as precursors to the thinking side and prepare the child for when parents introduce reasoning. Parents will talk about certain conditions to prepare the child for what lies ahead. For example, on a trip to the grocery store, the parent may caution the child to hold on to the cart. At this early stage in the child's life, it becomes an unalterable rule, and the parent may have a hard time convincing the child to let go of the cart when it's time to get into the car. Children at this age still don't understand that conditions are flexible and that once you are done using the cart, it's okay to let go. Children also believe the rules they live by are universal and become disturbed if they see other children not holding on to their carts. Thinking that adjusts for changing conditions and different rules is just beginning to develop.

Helping Your Child Through This Critical Stage

For a child learning to navigate the world, parents are the first and best teachers. Parents should be nurturing but firm, establish clear and concise rules of behavior, explain simply the need for these rules, and help their child understand the ramifications of breaking the rules. Rules, of course, should make sense and be age-appropriate. Rules should not be arbitrary, randomly enforced, or above a child's level of understanding.

The development of the thinking side in a child during this process takes patience and time. Some tactics used during this stage by parents are counterproductive and can actually interfere with the child's ability to move from impulse reacting to thinking. For example, parents sometimes use fear to motivate their child, as in "If you touch the knob on the stove, you'll get burned." Parents can unwittingly instill fear where there doesn't need to be fear and thus undermine important attempts by the child to explore the world safely and with a true understanding of risks and rewards.

Another trap for parents is being overly harsh, not understanding a child's limited capabilities for rational thought. It's easy to be overly harsh, especially when the basis for a rule is founded in part on a parent's own fear. Rules should be laid down in a soothing and sensible way, with a sound explanation for their existence. When children are aware of and understand what is expected of them, the parent-child relationship flows more smoothly.

Parents also may use threats to coerce their child into obeying a rule or listening to them. Many a parent has told their toddler, "I'm leaving right now. Bye," and then walked away. The unintentional result of this tactic can be to create in the child a fear of abandonment. The attempt to coerce the child into cooperating lays the foundation for insecurity.

Another trap at this stage in a child's development is the laissez-faire parent—a parent who doesn't provide sensitively placed coaching of the rules that govern behavior. These parents are overly indulgent of risk-taking behavior, or they remove all risks so the child never learns to deal with them. In this case, the child is given too wide of a berth at home and doesn't have the opportunity to develop self-limiting behavior.

School Years—the Social Environment

In school, the child enters a structured social environment with explicit and implicit rules governing social behavior and boundaries. The child must not only know these rules, but must understand them. In this environment, routine and repetition are key. The child understands that the rules are consistent and that adult responses don't change, so he or she must assimilate and display the expected behavior. The child learns through experience and watching others what is acceptable and what is out-of-bounds. The child also learns in school by reading about children beating their fears, overcoming their reacting side, loving their neighbors, and being loyal to their friends and family. These are all advanced building blocks for developing the child's thinking side and helping the child fit into the social structure present in the classroom.

At home, parents need to be attentive to the experiences their children are having in school. Relaying the events of the day helps a child process what has happened and gives the parent an opportunity to offer new viewpoints or interpretations. Reading stories also helps reinforce the rapid development the child's thinking side is undergoing. Stories can reflect what is going on in school—for example, dealing with a class bully—and refine the child's problem-solving abilities. A parent's volunteer involvement in the classroom also helps the parent to understand class dynamics, teacher expectations, and the environment in which the child must function.

The Thinking Side Prevails, But Not Always

The amazing development of children's reasoning abilities from the age of three, when they are still very reactive, to the abstract thinking skills of the six, seven, and eight year old is nothing short of amazing. Maturation gives children more and more layers of skills. They have a deeper understanding of situations and can think more abstractly to account for changing conditions. At three, they are still breaking all the rules, but at six, they are entirely different children, who can think for themselves. Yet some children have a more difficult time than others as they move from being a reacting toddler to a thinking grade-schooler.

A number of different scenarios, some temperamental, some environmental, and some neurological, can hold children back from fully developing their thinking side. For example, a child may be defiant, overly aggressive, or highly individualistic. A child may have an intrinsic neurological problem, such as ADHD (attention deficit hyperactivity disorder). Or, the child may have parents who did not challenge and help develop the child's thinking side in the early years, and thus the child simply did not have the opportunity to learn the needed skills.

In these difficult-to-coach children, the thinking side is not *absent;* it is simply *less available* because of the strong pull of impulse. These children are more challenging to coach than other children, but parents will find that if they use the Parent Coaching Cards in a way that fits their child's personality, they can help their child rein in the reacting side and keep the thinking side in control.

Coaching the Difficult-to-Coach Child

To kids with a more vulnerable self-esteem, coaching feels like criticizing. These children are hardened by life's experiences and take a jaded and cynical view of the Parent Coaching Cards. They may have parents who are yellers, or they may have had many disappointments in life or too many tough challenges thrown at them physically, emotionally, and academically. For these children, Parent Coaching Cards seem to add to the mountain of "life work" to which they already have to attend. Parents must be more thoughtful, creative, and careful if the Parent Coaching Cards are to be perceived as a useful tool and not as a punishment.

The first step for parents of these children is to recognize the right time to have a conversation. If the only time they engage their child in discussion is in the midst of anger, the child will quickly turn them off. These parents need to recognize that coaching is a two-way street, that the coach sometimes needs coaching too, and that they must share with their child their own mistakes. Without trust and respect, trying to coach the difficult-to-coach child is an exercise in futility.

So, what is the best way to approach these children? For some kids, a nonchalant approach works best. Make the cards a family project and take turns reading and discussing the cards at the dinner table. Or, set aside some time one night a week for a family discussion of a particular card as parents share stories and lessons from their own experiences. By using a family or group setting, the finger isn't pointing at any one person, but the one person who needs to hear the message does.

Once key card concepts are in place, such as **Find the Brakes!**, you can use them with your child in a nonthreatening manner. When said in a voice both firm and nurturing, a reminder such as **When Words Pop Out, Watch Out!** can do wonders to remind a child of a card's message and intent and to help the child regain control of his or her reacting side.

A bad time to read and discuss the whole text on a card is in the midst of or right after a crisis. The difficult-to-coach child is most resistant at this point, but he or she may be open to discussion a few hours later, when emotions have settled. The parent may start a conversation with something like, "Remember what happened when your team lost its game? I felt bad for you. I think we should talk about what happened." Sometimes, even coaching-resistant kids agree to turn to the cards after some pivotal negative event, such as an athletic disappointment, academic failure, or social humiliation.

It's also important not to use the Parent Coaching Cards in a way that embarrasses the child. A parent should not single out a child and say the child needs to work on a particular card, especially in front of a sibling or friend. If one-on-one coaching is what works best for your child, make sure to do it in a private area of your home. If you sense your child is beginning to tune you out, don't force the issue; just put the cards away and wait for another opportunity. Parents need to know when not to spring Parent Coaching Cards on their kids. If the difficult-to-coach child is experiencing a relatively calm and happy period, it may not be the best time to approach Parent Coaching Cards in a one-on-one setting. The child may resent the parent bringing up problems and reminding the child of difficult emotions and trying circumstances.

With any child—but especially with the difficult-to-coach child— timing and presentation of the Parent Coaching Cards can be everything. Some children are more forgiving of a parent's misattempts at coaching, while others will begin to build a wall against the very idea of Parent Coaching Cards. Parents must proceed with caution and be well tuned to their child's emotional state.

The Thinking Side and Reacting Side Card

This is the only card designed to be introduced first, as an instruction card that explains the purpose and format of Parent Coaching Cards. The title introduces fundamental concepts about teaching children to develop the ability to think through problems rather than automatically reacting to them. Many children will readily understand the difference between thinking and reacting sides while others will require more examples to clarify the distinctions.

Since grasping the concepts presented in the **Thinking Side and Reacting Side** card will have a great impact on the success of the entire system, parents are encouraged to commit the time necessary to ensure their child's comprehension. The card lends itself to Chalk Talks, with parents offering their own personal anecdotes or hypothetical situations and then asking the child whether the thinking or reacting side was in charge. You can invite your child to offer examples, or you can suggest actual situations from the child's life and then ask, "Which side do you think was in charge?" When facing a potential conflict with your child, talk aloud about your possible reactions, such as, "My reacting side wants me to keep arguing with you, but my thinking side realizes that will just push us further apart."

By helping your child develop a comprehensive understanding of his or her thinking and reacting sides, you can make it easier for your child to begin to experience how keeping a watch over behavior can help our lives go more smoothly. When the thinking side becomes the lifeguard of behavior, the need to rescue drowning emotions dwindles over time, and the child will become emotionally and socially stronger.

Chapter 3
CAN'T ALWAYS GET WHAT YOU WANT!

There are times in life when you get to visit great places, receive great gifts, and have great times with family and friends. These times fill you up with feelings of love and happiness. Then, there are times when **you don't get what you want.** You may end up feeling so angry and empty that it becomes tough to remember all the times you felt totally filled up. When this happens, your reacting side may cause you to hurt others with angry words and actions. But, this just causes more problems—like getting punished for your mean behavior.

To stop this cycle, read this talk-to-yourself message:

Sometimes I get what I want and sometimes I don't. Just like my favorite TV shows, even good things have built-in endings. My thinking side can prepare me for endings and the times I won't get what I want. I can decide to remember a favorite time when I felt really filled up. This happy memory of being filled with good feelings can help push away the angry and empty ones.

Endless Desires

Children today are bombarded with commercial messages that are turning them into consumers with appetites that never seem to be satiated. It's what some parents call the "Barbie® Syndrome"—you have the Barbie doll, but now your child "needs" the house, the hot tub, the pool, the car, a few of Barbie's friends, a new wardrobe, and on, and on, and on. Or, your child received a new video game system, but the desire for the latest game is perpetual. Parents become exasperated and feel that their children have little appreciation for anything, yet they also have a hard time saying no.

What's a parent to do? You can opt out of the current system and say you are never going to buy your kid any of that stuff, or you can return to Earth and help your child develop the emotional skills needed to handle desire and disappointment.

And disappointment is everywhere. Grocery stores, once solely the realm of food products, now vie with toy stores for your discretionary dollars. Few parents have taken their child to the grocery store and not heard "Can I have . . ." at least ten times. Gas stations dangle collectible baseballs by their cash registers. Fast-food restaurants sell toys as part of their combo meals. Bookstores are loaded with stuffed animals, games, gotta-have doodads, and lots of other nonliterary merchandise. At every corner and down every aisle, there will be something your child wants. Even more insidious is the friend whose parents buy their child everything, making your child feel the pressure to keep up.

A child's desires and wants may also take a noncommercial form—eating ice cream before dinner, arguing when it comes time to leave a party or the playground, or refusing to turn off the TV to do homework. All of these can trigger a child's reacting side, setting him or her up for frustration and anger when a parent denies a request.

Four-year-old Lauren's desire was to have friends over all the time. But Lauren was not satisfied with one friend—she often wanted four friends over at the same time. Lauren's mother, Beth, already had four children of her own and simply didn't want the chaos of eight children in her house every day—once in a while was plenty. She used the **Can't Always Get What You Want!** card with Lauren to remind her about the times she did get what she wanted and how she had more than one friend over just the day before. Before working with the card, Lauren was grumpy for a long time after being told "no," and Beth was frustrated. Now, she reminds Lauren to use her thinking side and to remember that she "can't always get what she wants." Lauren still gets grumpy when she doesn't get her way, Beth says, but the grumpiness lasts for just a minute and then Lauren moves on.

Beth used the central concept of the **Can't Always Get What You Want!** card to help Lauren move past feelings of frustration. The card encourages children to use their thinking side to remember times when they felt really filled up. This helps them handle disappointments and keep a bigger picture of how their lives are filled with good things.

Life's Early Frustrations

Frustration is the inability to get or do what you want, and it is one of the first emotions our children experience in early childhood with the introduction of delays (can't warm up that bottle fast enough); rules ("No!"); and denial of desire ("That's your brother's blankie"). Frustration intolerance is among the earliest roadblocks a child is forced to contend with on life's journey, and temperamental variables come into play, as do parents who are overly indulgent or ambivalent. Parents need to help their developing child contend with frustration—constant gratification delays the child's development of frustration tolerance, while constant denial can fill a child with neediness and dependency. A balance between frustration and gratification is important in creating tolerance in a child.

But the process of gratification and frustration is a difficult one for a child to understand. Early on, parents are typically the givers of gratification, yet to a child, it may seem that there is no rhyme or reason to a parent's decision. Yesterday, the child asked for a candy bar and was told no, but today the child was told yes. Or the child may throw a tantrum to get something he or she wants. Giving in reinforces the behavior, but the parent also fears that long walk off the plank—dragging a screaming, kicking child out of a store or restaurant while everyone else watches and judges.

Helping Your Child Develop a Tolerance for Disappointment

To a child, the parent is the gatekeeper of desires and satisfaction. With relatively little understanding of budgets and limitations, many children believe their parents can get them anything they want or let them do anything they want to do, but the parents simply choose not to.

The key to helping children develop frustration tolerance is to have in place clear rules that are consistently enforced. "Consistently" is the operative word here. There will, of course, be exceptions to the rules—giving surprises is fun for the parent and child and helps the child realize that gratification can sneak up on him when he least expects it—but explain clearly to your child that this is an exception and why you are making the exception. Some rules may include no buying toys or candy at the grocery store, no sweet snacks before dinner, no TV before homework is completed, and no playing with friends on Saturday until the child's bedroom is cleaned up. Having simple, well-communicated, and age-appropriate rules can go a long way to helping children understand that they don't always get what they want.

Even with rules, there are bound to be outbursts, and how parents handle these outbursts will help their child handle frustration. For example, if you are at the store with your child and he or she sees a new toy car that he or she absolutely must have, you have several choices. You can simply say OK and buy the car; you can say no and explain that today you're not at the store to buy cars; or, with an older child, you can suggest that the child needs to use his or her own money to buy the car.

Solution one, of course, is the easiest solution and provides the child with instant gratification. But, using solution one too much builds expectations in the child, so that when the adult wants to say no, the child will have a difficult time handling the disappointment. Solution two works, but the parent has to accept the consequences. Some children will simply shrug it off as a "never-hurts-to-ask" moment, while others will suffer a complete meltdown. Idle threats are not useful at times like these. Parents can use words to distract the child; give the child something else to hold on to; remind the child of the times he or she felt filled up ("We bought a car when we were here last week"); or do something interactive with the child, like trying out a new game. The parent replaces the gratification of the shopping center with his or her involvement with the child. Even with all that, there are times where you may just have to leave the store carrying a screaming child. Consider it an investment in creating a tolerant child who can eventually handle disappointment with more aplomb.

The best way children can learn that they can't always get what they want is for parents to set expectations from the beginning. Use the **Can't Always Get What You Want!** card to direct discussion about desires. Point to the boy's "I-want-it" bubble in the illustration and ask what might be in your child's bubble of desires. Such a Chalk Talk might sound like, "We are going to the toy store to buy a birthday present for Sarah. We are not going to buy anything for ourselves. Let's keep our thinking sides in control and not let our reacting sides take over when we get there." When the parent gets to the store, he or she will have to remind the child of why they are there and incorporate the child's help: "Why don't you pick out a card?"

Parents can also help curtail their child's overactive consumerism by having frequent discussions about wants and needs, how commercials create desire, and how the media influences our thinking. With older children, watch TV commercials together and discuss what the sales pitch is and what the reality of a certain product is compared to how it is presented on TV. Look at how programming and products are developed to keep children coming back for more. The culture of consumerism already exists, and parents must prepare their children for the inevitable pitches they will face everywhere they turn.

Can't Always Get What You Want, But That's OK!

Denying a child's request challenges his or her frustration tolerance, a vital emotional skill. It's common for a child's mood to suddenly become negative after being denied something. During these times, children find it hard to see the "big picture" of all that parents do provide, and, instead, they zero in on what they want at that moment. The **Can't Always Get What You Want!** card refocuses attention on those times when children felt filled up and helps them tolerate life's inevitable frustrations. The illustration on the card of the boy's thought bubble filled with "good stuff" offers parents the opportunity to ask their child what would be in his or her bubble. By thinking about what he or she already has and what has been done for him or her in the past, the child can get past temporary disappointments and move on to a more realistic appreciation of how filled up he or she really is.

Chapter 4
QUIT THE CLOWNING!

Clowning around seems fun and gets laughs. You may act silly to get attention or impress others, but it doesn't always work out that way. **Clowning around can backfire.** Sometimes it backfires at school, getting you in trouble with teachers. Sometimes it backfires with other kids, who think you're too weird to be around. This makes you feel bad about yourself and there's nothing funny about that!

The quicker you learn to **quit the clowning**, the quicker others will see you as mature and not so hungry for attention.

Turn off your silly side and turn on your thinking side by reading this talk-to-yourself message:

Silly behavior just doesn't blend with most people and places. Life goes much better when I act my age. **My clowning around** might make me and maybe a few other kids crack up laughing, but it wrecks my chances with most people. My thinking side can help me keep a lid on the silliness and help me know when it's perfectly okay to clown around. I can learn more mature ways of getting noticed by watching how non-silly kids do it.

Born Entertainers

Almost every child clowns around from time to time. They do goofy things, tell silly jokes, or make fun of others, especially when they are in groups with their peers. Most clowning around is harmless, but some children clown too much. The power of a child's social group can be very strong, strong enough to unleash normally dormant aspects of the child's personality. As these children try to fit in and make people laugh, they can sometimes create a social stigma for themselves by misreading their environment and "delivering" inappropriate material at inappropriate times. These children often fail to understand the subtle social dynamics of the world around them, and they don't pay attention to other factors that give them clues about the appropriateness of their behavior.

A child's behavior is sometimes a result of his or her current situation. When children are standing in the lunch line at school, waiting at the table for dinner, or standing by in the classroom as papers are handed out, they might clown around to entertain themselves. A child may clown to get attention, or a child may clown to get some social payback. If children can entertain and make others laugh with their antics, they perceive that their social status is lifted. This type of clowning can backfire, though, when other children consider the behavior as too mean-spirited, odd, or overly dramatic. Or a group might not favor clowning because everyone may suffer the consequences if a teacher or parent has to intervene.

It's a Geography Joke

Like most humor, clowning often doesn't travel well. When adults say, "Well, it's a geography joke," they mean that you had to be there to get it. This idea is similar to what children experience— what's funny at one place may be frowned on in another—and it can be tough for kids who struggle with social nuances to figure out. Parents can help their children understand how context affects clowning.

For example, within a child's small social group there is a certain give-and-take that accommodates the child's behavior. The child receives feedback from and gives feedback to friends, and there is an implicit social understanding among the group's members. The child becomes conditioned by the smaller social group that particular clowning behaviors are not only okay but also desirable.

If the child tries the same behavior in another environment, it may not be acceptable. This situation is true for children who are taken out of their family environment where certain behavior is tolerated. For example, a 6-year-old-boy looks up to and adores his 14-year-old brother. The older child gets great satisfaction from making the younger child laugh, and his antics are designed to appeal to his brother. When he takes this clowning to his social group, they may laugh at first, but, in reality, his behavior embarrasses his friends and can ostracize him from his peers.

Children need to take the time to develop an understanding of what the clues are in their environment so they can adjust their behavior accordingly. Children can use the **Quit the Clowning!** card to help them put their thinking side in charge and ask themselves: "Who is present? How well do I know these people? What will the effect of clowning be on the people around me? Is this a good place to say or do something funny?"

Coaching Social Awareness

Coaching children to appreciate how their surroundings affect their behavior begins, like most things, at home. Parents need to make an effort to instill in their children an appreciation of how circumstances determine appropriate behavior. Early on, they must help their children become good social observers by helping them understand social dynamics.

Talk with your child about clues and instructions—how to take clues from the environment and then take instructions from those clues. Try a Chalk Talk with your child to anticipate situations and head off clowning behavior that won't be appreciated. For example, in the following Chalk Talk, a family is going to a relative's house for dinner. The child's cousins seem to bring out extreme clowning behavior.

> **Mom:** I'd like to talk before we leave for Uncle Bobby's house about clowning around and what's OK and what's not. Do you remember what happened when we were there a couple of weeks ago?

> **Son:** Yeah, Uncle Bobby got mad at me for joking around when he was talking about something serious.

> **Mom:** I know you really like joking around with your cousins, but it seems like sometimes you don't pay attention to what's going on around you. You go too far and don't know where to stop. Clowning is fun, but last time it backfired. What do you think you can do differently this time?

> **Son:** Well, I guess I could try not to be too silly—and not make fun of Uncle Bobby.

> **Mom:** I think that's a good start. Just remember to keep your thinking side turned on and not let your clowning ruin your fun.

Chalk Talks about clowning should help parents train their kids to key in on clues and instructions and to improve their vision of social circumstances. Using Chalk Talks, parents encourage their kids to think ahead, not just respond to the moment. By doing this, parents show their children how to expand their social repertoire and develop other ways they can get positive social attention.

When kids have gotten in trouble for their social clowning, parents have to be careful not to punish them if they simply don't know how to be accepted in the normal sense—how to make deposits in the social "bank" that will show a positive return. Punishment can harm children's developing self-esteem, and they may come to view themselves as "damaged." Rather, parents should use their coaching skills to be corrective and coach their kids on positive ways to get attention.

Clowning Costs Kids

Children may not always understand the hidden social costs of their behavior, and parents should have an open and honest conversation about just how much clowning can cost. Parents can help their children understand that they are judged by their peers and the adult world, based on their maturity and behavior: "Out-of-control clowning might mean you don't get invited to parties or sleepovers, or it might make your friends want to spend less time with you." Kids who clown too much can unwittingly put barriers on the path to friendships, success in school, and contentment within the family. Children who do not learn to discern the finer social nuances surrounding their clowning behavior can continue these character traits into adulthood, where they may become social pariahs—loud, boisterous, constantly interrupting others, telling inappropriate jokes—the proverbial bull in the china shop.

Quit the Clowning!

Many children attempt to entertain peers with silly behavior but are unaware of the resulting social outcomes. If they get laughs, it may appear that their clowning is being met with approval by peers. Yet sometimes a peer is simply laughing and not necessarily liking the person responsible for the behavior.

The **Quit the Clowning!** card identifies the negative impression clowning leaves in the minds of other children as well as adults. It's useful to point to how the expressions of the two girls in the illustration capture how clowning often backfires. Parents can then take the card a step further by suggesting, "Getting laughs for acting silly may get you noticed, but it doesn't get you friends."

Chapter 5
WHEN WORDS POP OUT, WATCH OUT!

How many times has this happened to you? You're bugged by something going on. Maybe you feel angry and before you know it, words **pop out** that land you in deep trouble. Or, something seems kind of funny and before you know it, you say something as a joke. Another person, usually an adult, like a parent, teacher, or coach, doesn't agree about the funny part. It doesn't even help to say, "I was just kidding around."

These situations happen when wrong words **pop out** before your thinking side can decide if it's really a good idea to say them.

Read this talk-to-yourself message to learn how to stop wrong words from causing trouble:

It's okay to share ideas and feelings, as long as I choose the right time and right words. When I let my reacting side speak for me, wrong words usually **pop out**. These wrong words lead me to time-out or some other punishment. My thinking side can help me find the right words, or remind me that sometimes I just need to keep quiet. I can be on the lookout and stop wrong words before they **pop out**.

I Hate You!

More than one parent has been on the receiving end of their child's anguished "I hate you!" and it's not fun. Trish was one such parent. Her daughter Shelby, age eight, let words pop out with little regard for what they were and where they fell. When Shelby would ask for something and was told no, Trish says Shelby would "completely freak out" and start yelling, "I hate you!" Trish was struggling with this aspect of her daughter's behavior when a friend told her about the Parent Coaching Cards her son had been introduced to at a camp for troubled kids. Though Trish knew her daughter's behavior was pretty normal, she was intrigued, so she ordered the cards and went right to **When Words Pop Out, Watch Out!**

Shelby started learning about the cards' messages by coloring in the illustrations on the cards. As she colored, she and her mom would discuss the pictures. Eventually, they came around to a discussion about the picture of the embarrassed boy on the **When Words Pop Out, Watch Out!** card. Shelby and her mom talked about inappropriate words and how they could hurt others and get the speaker into trouble. Shelby became aware of when words were popping out and began to focus on changing those words. But turnabout is fair play: One day, when Trish said an inappropriate word, a small voice replied, "Mom, when words pop out, watch out!"

Where Did You Hear That Word?

When children are young, they act largely on impulse. Their feelings are easily triggered by their environment, and frustration tolerance tends to be low, easily challenged by a request being denied and other situations. Highly reactive tendencies are very common, and parents tend to make allowances given the age of their children. Children can toss out an inappropriate word, a hurtful statement, or an unfeeling comment and most parents will respond with, "We don't use words like that in our family," as a way of teaching their children what is and is not acceptable language.

When children reach school age, they are expected to better censor what they say. School, family life, and peer relationships help children understand appropriate language limits. But some children have trouble inhibiting their impulsive speech. Like the boy on the Parent Coaching Card, such children know after they've let something pop out that it was the wrong thing to say, but they lack the skills to stop themselves from saying it.

These children often are more competitive, sensitive, or achievement-oriented than other children. They bring to life a strong intensity, and this "fuel" can cause wrong words to pop out, creating trouble in their lives. Parents usually are aware of a child's temperamental tendencies in this area but often don't know how to manage it or change it, beyond using time-outs or taking away favorite things.

Complicating things for these children is the nature of the environment that surrounds them. Not only are children having trouble censoring themselves, it seems that the entire world is having trouble using appropriate language. Curse words are sprinkled liberally throughout family TV shows and movies, popular music, on the radio, and in the school hallways, and this has a normalizing effect on inappropriate language. Parents and older siblings often don't censor their language and, many times, are the first off-color-language instructors in a child's life.

I Was Just Kidding Around

Using words to try to bolster one's social standing is a pretty common tactic for children interacting with each other. In our culture, people are used to kidding each other with what they consider witty and funny comments that can actually be very hurtful. Taking their cues from grown-ups, children use the same tact. Children use inappropriate humor regardless of the feelings of others. A hurtful comment is followed by an "I was just kidding around," "I didn't mean it," or "I was only teasing," meaningless phrases that don't take the sting out of barbed comments. In families, this type of verbal baiting tends to be deliberate. Children may take advantage of opportunities to get a dig in, or to turn the tables on a sibling. What they often don't understand is that the good feeling they get from "busting" on their brother or sister is only temporary and comes at a cost to their long-term relationship.

Socially, such behavior is risky because it can be seen by others as cruel rather than funny. These aren't kids who typically want to bully or hurt others but, rather, kids who perceive that a social advantage is gained from putting others down. They like the laughs their comments often elicit from their peers, especially at the expense of others.

Helping Your Child Develop Verbal Control

The **When Words Pop Out, Watch Out!** card grew out of the need for kids to develop verbal inhibition. They need to develop the place where thought mediates spoken language, the place for kids to reflect on how even jokes, if expressed at the wrong time and place, can get somebody into trouble. The message of the card is that children should get into the habit of thinking to themselves, "Is this something I should say right now?" and develop self-monitoring that keeps them from making insensitive comments to another child. This is a critical social skill, especially in the minds of parents, teachers, and other children. If your child has a reputation for dishing out rude comments, making jokes in poor taste, or using inappropriate language, it carries a great deal of weight when others make a determination about his or her character.

This notion of character and reputation is also an important one for children with verbal impulsivity to grasp. They often don't understand that other people carry a mental picture of them, a picture that continues to be drawn, and that what a child says is the most critical part of this mental picture in the minds of others. Even one very poorly placed comment can be recalled months and even years later. Parents need to communicate just how critical it is for kids to find the brakes for verbal impulsivity, to put their thinking side in control of their words. This is crucial to success in the social world.

Home is the best place to begin practicing a "watch over words." Kids let words pop out easily at home because of the safety they feel there. Many children are very well controlled outside of the home but, at home, are far more reactive to siblings and parents. Parents can help their children gain more control by having a Chalk Talk about triggers and traps that cause them to lose control over their words. If a child's verbal impulsivity is not adequately controlled at home, it will become even more reactive over the years.

Controlling verbal impulsivity takes practice, and there are some good tools and games parents can use to help their child develop word control. A good place to start with your child is the ABCs. ABC stands for:

A: Aware I want to say something.

B: Take a breath.

C: Control what I say.

For example, if a child has just had an incident where he or she couldn't control his or her words, the parent may want to take the time after the child has calmed down to relive what happened and to talk out some other options. Here's a Chalk Talk example:

Dad: You let your words pop out. I understand why—it's frustrating when your brother breaks your LEGOs®.

Son: He makes me so mad; I can't help what I say sometimes.

Dad: I understand you were angry, but that doesn't mean you have to let those words pop out. Listen to your thinking voice. Ask yourself, "Is this a good thing to say right now?" It sounds like you didn't ask yourself that question. Or, if you did, you didn't get the right answer.

Son: I didn't ask that question because I was too mad.

Dad: Well, next time, try to remember your ABCs. Be aware that you want to say something, then take a breath and control what you say. Can you think of how you would talk differently with your little brother if you had the chance to do it again?

Son: Well, I might say I don't want him to play with my LEGOs without my permission. Or I might ask you for help.

Dad: Those are both really good ideas.

Parents help their children more when they take corrective, rather than punitive, action. Helping children think about how they could have changed their past behavior can help them control their future behavior. Another way to help your child visualize verbal control is to make examples of characters in books or TV shows. Chalk Talk with your child about what a character said and how the character got into trouble, and then have your child think of some other dialogue that may have resulted in a better outcome. Look for the words that hurt others and see if your child can understand the emotions of a character who has been harmed by someone else's words.

Of course, it's hard for kids to learn self-control skills if parents lack them. It's important that parents talk objectively about their own word problems and let their child know they are sorry for inappropriate language or hurtful comments. Tell your child that it is important for you to teach him or her how to deal with anger and that you pledge to work harder and take responsibility when you do make mistakes. Many parents feel awkward and vulnerable when confronted with the idea of apologizing or working to change their own behavior. This is new territory for a lot of parents, but it's a great place to start. It brings the relationship with the child back into a positive mode of communication.

When Words Pop Out, Watch Out!

Verbal impulsivity is a common problem at home and school. The illustration on the Parent Coaching Card of the boy who has caught himself too late captures the dilemma of many children who don't think before they speak. Life can easily turn toward conflict when children say the "wrong" things. But harsh parental reactions don't help a child manage verbal impulsivity. Instead, such reactions may quickly escalate the conflict if the child is the type who fights fire with fire and words with words.

Prepare yourself to hear wrong words from time to time. When this happens, try to respond with a firm cautionary warning like, "Beware of words that pop out of your mouth." Getting into the habit of doing this diminishes the unintended effect of overreacting. When we overreact to wrong words, we implicitly send the message that such words have power over adults. By doing this, you practically guarantee that you will hear these words again when your child is feeling particularly powerless against adult authority.

A more prudent approach is to resist "letting them have it" verbally and, instead, to have them wrestle with what they said. By not injecting your own anger into the encounter, you provide an opportunity for your child's conscience to become activated. In this case, feelings of guilt can "mark" the lesson; an apology may even be offered later. Work with children to help them develop control over their verbal impulses by practicing the ABCs, by encouraging them to keep their thinking sides in control, by revisiting situations that got them into trouble, and by helping them learn better ways to communicate their emotions through words that help, rather than words that hurt.

Chapter 6
STEP INTO YOUR CANTALOUPE SKIN!

There are loads of things in life that can upset you—being teased, having trouble with homework, not being invited to a party, and other stuff like that. When you have your "banana skin" on, you easily **feel bruised**. You probably spend time feeling bad and acting angry. Sometimes your reacting side makes you want to hurt others back so you're not the only one feeling crummy. But this only makes things worse.

If you see something that bruises heading your way, try dealing with it by reading this talk-to-yourself message:

I can't expect success all the time. Hard times are a part of everyone's life. I must remember that although I feel bad when things don't work out, I am not a bad person. I do plenty of things just fine and people notice my strengths. I need to remember my successes right now, the pride I can feel, and all the good things others believe about me. **I can use this pride and grow a thicker "cantaloupe skin"** to prepare for what's coming. My thinking side will help me do this.

What Kind of Skin Is Your Child In?

When it comes to handling adversity, it seems that most children come into the world prewired to react in a certain way. We all know the child that brushes off the most biting insult or slight without the least reaction—the child who seems unfazed at being left out, content to go on her way and about her business. And, at the other extreme, we also know the child who seems as fragile as an icicle on a warm winter's day—melting away when the heat is on. These children often take innocent teasing to heart, react out of proportion to a perceived slight, and basically live much of their childhoods as the walking emotionally wounded.

Susan and her husband, David, often talk with their son, Chris, about what it means to have a "banana skin"—thin and easily bruised. As a family, they discuss how David's "skin" is more sensitive than his wife's and how this affects his reactions to those around him. Chris, age nine, shares with his parents how his reacting side takes over when a friend says something hurtful or how it stings when it seems like everyone but him gets invited to a birthday party. Susan likes how their family discussions about the cantaloupe skin card have helped Chris have a better understanding of his own times of feeling hurt and how he can better protect himself against such hurts in the future—how he can use his thinking side to develop his own cantaloupe skin.

The **Step Into Your Cantaloupe Skin!** card is commonly used with children who are sensitive to the point of being unable to handle everyday emotional bumps and bruises, a condition they express with emotional outbursts, blame, and withdrawal from activities. Underneath most banana skins are children with feelings of inadequacy that leave them vulnerable to the everyday assaults life throws at them.

These children often are their own worst enemies, because their own negative thoughts can become self-fulfilling prophecies, leading to additional frustrations and feelings of inadequacy. A parent can help to replace those negative thoughts by pulling out something the child is really proud of, an accomplishment he or she was able to achieve. This reminds the child how he or she overcame something difficult in the past and can do it again.

Exploring How Oversensitivity Can Develop

The origins of oversensitivity often are linked to temperament but also to parents who are overindulgent and don't inoculate their child with a dose of frustration every once in a while early in life. This inoculation is a result of the balance between frustration and gratification. For example, doing a child's homework for him or her doesn't build in a level of frustration tolerance that helps the child develop patience for working toward a solution. Likewise, trying to give a child everything he or she desires fails to promote the ability to process disappointment in a healthy manner when there is something the child can't have. Balancing "Yes, I'll help with this" with "No, I'd like you to work on this for a while," and "Yes, I think it's OK to buy this" with "No, we aren't buying toys today," helps the child develop a resilient cantaloupe skin that will protect him or her further down the line.

Keeping this balance in mind helps children build resilience. Overly gratified children don't experience enough frustration, and so they don't deal well with it later in life. When they are involved with school, friendships, and other social situations, these children can crumble under the pressure of feeling frustrated. If parents always button their child's coat because the child gets too frustrated to do it, the child will be crushed upon reaching a certain age and finding that his peers are buttoning their coats and he can't. Instead, if parents give their child a few minutes of frustration each day in learning to button the coat, then their child will be more resilient and ready to handle challenging situations when venturing out into the world beyond the parents' protective custody.

This can be difficult for some parents to do. They feel that they always have to leave their child with a sense of satisfaction, otherwise they are bad parents. But finding that balance between over-gratification and frustration is important in helping a child become resilient. Parents who allow a child to cry out of frustration give their child a chance to grow in his or her capacity to endure frustration.

Helping a Child Turn Banana Skin Into Cantaloupe Skin

For Gail, helping her 15-year-old son, Brandon, shed his banana skin was an important part of his becoming more mature. Brandon was "very sensitive—overly sensitive—very self-centered and couldn't see beyond his own needs." Gail used the **Step Into Your Cantaloupe Skin!** card with him frequently, first reviewing the card and discussing it as it fit his personality, then engaging strategies outlined in the card to help him grow a cantaloupe skin. Brandon learned to remember his successes when he saw something bruising heading his way, or, if it was too late to protect himself, he was able to recover more quickly by telling himself that even though he was a good person, bad things happen once in a while.

Understanding what triggers your child's reacting side and exposes his or her banana skin is a good place to start when building a cantaloupe skin. Some kids simply don't handle certain situations very well. For example, a child who perceives herself as not very good at basketball may just walk away when friends start to play. Another child who doesn't think he is a very good student may blow a spelling test simply because of reinforced self-doubt.

Parents can help their child build resilience in select sensitive areas by focusing on his or her core strengths. For instance, if your child is an excellent speller but loses it when he or she gets one wrong on a test, you can help adjust your child's perspective by emphasizing all of the questions he or she got right. Parents should also help kids understand what it means to feel empowered in social situations, for them to have a powerful view of self and not let other people's mean words penetrate their cantaloupe skin.

Children, with the help of their parents, can employ the idea of "Power Talk," using words to protect themselves and deflect hurt coming from others. For example, if a child just got braces and is worried about the reactions of classmates, parents can have a Chalk Talk with the child to help him develop a Power Talk script to handle any comments from other kids. These can range from a simple "Thanks for noticing," to a humorous "Gee, I didn't know you were the braces reporter," to a clever, "Yeah, when I was getting them put on I got to watch a movie with special video glasses. It was really cool!" The point is to talk with children ahead of time and help them develop some responses. Encourage in them an understanding that withdrawing, looking down, or "shrinking" in size doesn't help them at all. Eye contact and body posture are important parts of cantaloupe skin.

Setting Expectations

Kids with banana skins often bruise when something or someone, themselves included, doesn't meet their expectations. For example, if a child had a great soccer game with lots of scoring and a team victory, he or she may expect that at the next game, too. But if they get beat, the child freaks out. Children often expect prior performance to predict future performance. If they set the bar too high, their self-esteem can suffer when results fall below that bar. They may begin to display poor sportsmanship, or they may withdraw from a sport they previously enjoyed. Parents can help their children through these times by talking about being realistic and having a Chalk Talk about what to expect. The child can't always be the star. Her team won't always win. The child should focus instead on being prepared for the game, doing her best, and using the thinking side to help her play with cantaloupe skin on.

Parents also can use their own experiences to highlight how they use resiliency skills to get through tough situations. For example, if a police car pulls you over, you can later discuss with your child how embarrassed and ashamed you felt for doing something wrong, but how you then used your cantaloupe skin to accept the criticism (and the ticket) the police officer gave to you. It's important for children to understand that they will handle plenty of things fine in their daily lives, but occasionally they will make mistakes, others will pick on them, or they won't perform to their expectations. And that's OK.

Step Into Your Cantaloupe Skin!

Many children overreact to disappointing events or hurtful situations. Their reacting sides take over and prevent their thinking sides from putting the situation in perspective. Feelings of intense anger, extreme tearfulness, frustration, and withdrawal are all common reactions in banana-skin children who have difficulty mustering up emotional resilience.

Parents can help by first identifying common triggers and preparing the child ahead of time when they know something bruising is heading their child's way. Next, they can help fortify their child's self-esteem by reminding the child of a recent success. These good feelings can help the child step into cantaloupe skin and face whatever comes his or her way. Parents can use a Chalk Talk to help their child develop Power Talks that will help him handle difficult situations. Parents also can share stories from their own lives, modeling how resilience helped them and how having a banana skin set them up to get hurt.

Chapter 7
DON'T TAKE THE BAIT!

Life is filled with all sorts of situations that may lead to trouble. Things may happen at a friend's house, when you're playing outside with a group, while watching TV with a brother or sister, or even at school. Maybe someone calls you a name or dares you to follow him into bad behavior. Maybe you see some dangerous fun that's hard to resist.

If you let them, **these situations will bait you**—just like a hooked worm baits a fish. Before you even know it, you've been **baited into** wrong action or a bad decision.

You may not even know you've taken the bait until it's too late, so it's a good idea to review this talk-to-yourself message from time to time:

I have to be on the lookout so I don't get **baited into** behaving badly. Getting **baited** can happen anytime, anywhere—and with anybody. One way to prevent this from happening is to stop and ask myself, "Am I being **baited** right now?"

If the answer is "yes," or even "maybe," stop. Do not follow the other person's lead. Don't let yourself react to whatever is happening at that moment. Give yourself time to think it through some more or to talk the situation over with someone you trust. **Don't take the bait!**

It's Hard Not to Take the Bait

Jeremy's grandmother, Sandra, is very involved in her grandson's life and was well aware that Jeremy, age nine, was having a problem with "taking the bait." In school, when kids would go outside for recess and "run wild" for a while, they would encourage Jeremy to join them. The problem was that the other kids could stop and Jeremy couldn't. Or, when classmates would bait him with teasing, Jeremy couldn't hold back his anger. Almost every day in school, he was getting into trouble.

When Sandra first brought home the Parent Coaching Cards, Jeremy came over after school every day and spent a week reading different cards. **Don't Take the Bait!** was one he returned to again and again. Sandra says it's a card they discussed daily, and Jeremy could begin to see that "taking the bait" was getting him in trouble. He worked on the talk-to-yourself message and, as a result, has been able to stop and ask himself, "Am I being baited right now?" The card helped Jeremy use his thinking side to realize when he was being baited and to get out of the situation before his reacting side got him into trouble. Jeremy still gets baited occasionally, Sandra says, but the improvement has been impressive.

Hook, Line, and Sinker

Don't Take the Bait! is a card that deals with social judgment and making better choices in the environment that surrounds a child. This is a social skill that is underdeveloped in many children. The card describes how the environment can trigger reactions, for better or worse. A lot of "circuitry" is involved when a child is tempted to take the bait: The power of peer groups; the intensity of impulses, curiosity, and intrigue; and the desire to retaliate, probe, or explore can all lead to bad outcomes.

Baiting comes in many different forms, including teasing, daring, taunting, and pressure to conform to the peer group. A child may be dared into doing something illegal or dangerous like stealing candy from a store or taking a sled down a hilly road. Children may be taunted into fighting or teased into retaliation, and they may also take the bait to fit into their peer group—"We're all making prank phone calls, why can't you?" Whatever form it takes, baiting often results in a bad outcome for the child. So, why do kids do it? Much of it is simple impulsivity—not stopping long enough to think or even consider consequences. Much of it also has to do with a desire to fit in and be liked, even when taking the bait can have unseen social costs. **Don't Take the Bait!** helps parents teach their children what types of bait they are attracted to and how to detect when they are being baited. Parents can help their children develop awareness so they don't take the bait.

Looking at the World Around Them

Some children have greater degrees of impulsivity and fewer coping skills than other children. The environment often pushes their buttons, and they respond inappropriately. Parents can explain to their children how they let the people and things around them control their behavior, rather than being in control of it themselves. One form of Chalk Talk might be to practice an innocent game of basketball and then throw in some teasing, one of the most common forms of baiting. If your child takes the bait and reacts with anger or withdrawal, you can point out how a different response might help him or her deal with such situations. Instead of getting mad, the child can ignore the teasing. Instead of withdrawing, the child can laugh with the teaser or turn the teasing around. For example, if your daughter is at school and another child is teasing her about how she plays soccer, she might try to turn it around by making it into a conversation: "Why don't we play, and maybe I'll learn a few things from you?"

Children can also be more direct in their attempts to stop teasing so they don't take the bait. An empowered verbal response can more quickly stem the tide of teasing than simply ignoring it. For example, your child can tell another child, "I don't want to be your enemy," and then direct the conversation into another area. This type of Power Talk helps a child build a sense of self-protection. Parents can practice with their children to help them develop a repertoire of ready responses when someone tries to bait them. For example, if a child tries to bait your child into pulling the fire alarm, your child can respond with, "I grew out of that stuff in second grade." Another common scenario is the child who shows up at school with a new pair of glasses and has to respond to teasing or comments about them. A good response might be, "It's my new movie-star look," or "Yeah, I'm getting used to it." Kids should approach baiting with a sense of humor that allows them to laugh at themselves and get out of situations gracefully.

Why Some Kids Bait

You know that your child struggles with taking the bait, but what about the kids who set the bait? Most baiters do it for social prestige and to do something in front of others that might get a laugh. Baiting might allow them to gain the upper hand over someone they feel inferior to in other areas. Some of these children may feel empty or inadequate and cover up by inflicting pain on others. Help your child understand these kids and realize that they may have some kind of plan for your child—usually bad—and does your child really want to be a part of that plan? It's important to impress upon your child that people who have been in trouble often lead others into trouble.

Siblings can also be baiters, and they are particularly good at pushing their brother's or sister's buttons and provoking a fight. Classic sibling baits include imitating, repeating, touching, teasing, and taking. Close proximity and time together can make sibling baiting particularly difficult to resolve. Add to that the emotional involvement of the parents, and baiting takes on a new dimension. But the basic responses are the same: stop and think before you act, Power Talk, turn the teasing around, use humor, and refuse to participate.

Even adults can be tricky baiters for children. Parents, relatives, and friends of the family are often guilty of teasing children in what they think is a good-natured way. Helping your child develop Power Talk answers and the ability to address adults rather than shrinking away can help your child deal with these situations while still being respectful. For example, an adult might say, "So, who's your girlfriend in school?" to which the child might respond, "I'll let you know when I meet her." Chalk Talk different scenarios with your child to help him or her get comfortable with a variety of replies.

Associating with baiters, especially in their peer group, does have social costs for children. Their reputations are only as good as the last thing people remember about them. The perception of a child's good character can be tarnished by an isolated event that lingers in people's memories for months or even years. If your child takes the bait, negative outcomes can color people's opinions. People tend to generalize about the nature of a person and may not be very forgiving or forgetting of even one mistake. Taking the bait can have lifelong negative consequences for children, and parents need to discuss this with their children. One great tool is the newspaper, where real-life stories of people taking the bait appear almost daily. Examples might include a teenager who was driving drunk, a boy who was dared to walk out on a frozen lake by his friends, or a girl who got lost in the woods after participating in a practical joke. Books you read with your children can also help point out how characters face the consequences of taking the bait.

Don't Take the Bait!

Social situations often test a child's ability to display adequate social judgment. Children may be easily provoked by siblings, peers, or even adults. Your child may also find it difficult to resist the social temptation to misbehave. Sometimes children's competitive or oversensitive natures make them prime candidates for being baited by others. The **Don't Take the Bait!** card helps children understand how to avoid these predicaments by revealing how others will attempt to bait them into reacting. Parents can use the illustration on the front of the card to brainstorm with their child about the kind of bait he or she finds hard to resist. Children feel more powerful when they can overcome their reacting side and use specific responses like, "Sorry, I'm not taking the bait." By not taking the bait, they show that they are in control of their lives and that they have the power to make good decisions.

Chapter 8

SHOW YOUR LOVE FOR PEOPLE, NOT JUST FOR STUFF!

Life is filled with all kinds of stuff to do and see—great toys, awesome video games, cool TV shows, and fun activities. These things can make you feel good and totally filled up while doing them. That's OK! Having fun is one of the terrific things about life. **But, it's not the only thing.**

Sometimes your interest in stuff can cause you to close off from people. That's not good for you and doesn't make them feel so great, either.

If your mind gets trapped in a tunnel of stuff, read this talk-to-yourself message as a reminder to keep showing your love for others:

Even though great stuff makes me feel filled up, all fun stops at some point. But **my love for others and their love for me doesn't ever end**. It's always there, deep inside, even though I might not be thinking about it. My thinking side can help me out of a tunnel of stuff. My thinking side reminds me to find ways to **show my love**—taking time to talk with my family, give hugs, write a note, or do something helpful without being asked.

In an Age of Consumption, Relationships Can Suffer

One hundred years ago, most children had little in their lives except their relationships with family and friends. Now, children have so much more "stuff" competing for their attention that many of these important relationships seem less important. Obsession with things like toys, video games, and computers can create a tunnel vision that ignores relationships. Children become so absorbed in their stuff that they lose focus on what's really valuable in their lives. When kids are too plugged into activities, they can become emotionally vacant inside—nobody's at home.

The **Show Your Love for People, Not Just for Stuff!** card focuses on helping children understand that all this stuff may be fun, but they can't forget the importance of nurturing the bonds between themselves and others. Parents can use the card to encourage their kids to use their thinking side to get them out of their "tunnel of stuff" and to remind them of ways to develop relationships with friends and family. Take time to review the illustration with your child and talk about what's in his or her tunnel of stuff and how the two boys in the picture can turn their backs on all that fun stuff to enjoy their friendship.

Love of Stuff Starts Early

Children as young as three and four years old can show the beginnings of an overly possessive orientation—they want their stuff, they don't want anybody else touching their stuff, and they would rather play alone than with others. Their manner of play sets up borders and reflects a deep desire for personal space. This is particularly true for only children and first-born children who grow accustomed to calling the shots early on and can develop overly strong attachments to their material goods.

Parents sometimes reinforce strong attachments to stuff as a way to protect the child's boundaries from siblings. A good way to prevent over-the-top possessiveness right off the bat is to downplay the notion of ownership. Boys and girls and brothers and sisters should share, and families as a whole should model sharing. Boundaries are okay when siblings are younger—mainly for damage control—but restrictions should change as children grow and learn to be more respectful of the work and activities of others.

Less Attached to Stuff, More Attached to People

As children grow, they usually become more attached to friends and less attached to things. Parents often express concern when their son or daughter is in middle childhood and prefers to stay at home by himself or herself rather than play with other kids. For many of these children, it's really not all that much fun to play with other children. There is a lot of frustration built into the experience. If they play by themselves, they get everything to themselves, accomplish things by themselves, and there is no give-and-take. This type of solitary play may be preferred. Playing with other children means dealing with a lot more emotions and negotiation, and some kids just don't want to make that effort or deal with the emotional hassle.

The Chalk Talk job of the parent here is to explain to the child what is taking place and how the pleasures in the child's life are tilted toward solitary pursuits. That may feel good now, but down the road, the child will want to have more balance as well as the ability to relate well with others and develop strong friendships. Parents can use the notion of a continuum to help their child understand that most people are happiest when their lives are in a balance—we all need alone time, and we all need time with other people.

A good place to start is to relate to how your child feels when he or she is left out. Explain that the child might prefer playing alone, but wonderful things can come by allowing other people to come into his or her life. Being a member of a group—being included—feels pretty good, too. You can begin to plant the seed that helps kids understand the problem. Help children begin to define fun differently. Rather than playing a computer game, building with LEGOs, or watching TV, they can look at fun as having a friend over and creating something together. Children stuck in their tunnels of stuff tend to be too oriented toward their own accomplishments and not toward the fun they can have with a friend. They tend to look at play dates with a cost-benefit analysis, seeing what they got out of it and what it cost them. Rather than saying, "Max and I had a nice time playing football together," they might say, "Max and I played football with some other kids, and he hardly ever passed to me. I don't really like playing with him."

Children who tend to socially isolate themselves also tend to want to be in control when they are with a group of children. Parents can use the **Show Your Love for People, Not Just for Stuff!** card to help their children understand that when they approach a group of friends, they don't have to be in charge, they don't have to be the best, and they don't have to win to have fun. They do need to turn off the filters that make them quantify playing as good or bad, win or lose, and realize they can just have fun being with their friends.

Stretch Your Child Into New Relationships

Many children feel very comfortable with the relationships within their family and in their own home. They feel fine showing their love for and relating to people within their own family, but they can't "stretch" that feeling to friendships and other relationships outside of the home. The family is nurturing and warm and doesn't make a lot of social demands. These kids can have a very narrow comfort zone and are easily inhibited or intimidated when outside of that zone, so naturally, they prefer being on their own at home where they have more control. These kids can talk a blue streak at home, where they are in their comfort zone, but then act completely different outside of the home. There is a lot of self-questioning going on, and strong emotional forces can cause a child to clam up verbally and emotionally.

In these situations, many parents exacerbate the problem by rescuing their child. If the child is asked a question, the parent will answer. Or a child may be afraid to make a phone call, and the parent makes it for the child. Parents need to help their children expand their social comfort zones by working with them on their social skills. The best way to stretch your child's abilities is to practice in a safe place. For example, your child may practice having a conversation with an understanding older cousin. Rehearse phone conversations with your child or do a Chalk Talk about what he or she might say to a stranger in the checkout line at the grocery store. A sample Chalk Talk might be:

Mom: You know how whenever we are in the checkout line at the grocery store, someone always makes a comment about your red hair?

Daughter: That makes me embarrassed.

Mom: I can tell it does, because you usually shrink away behind me. But I think I can help you. What if we practice and think of some things that you could say back to that person—things that might even put a smile on the person's face?

Daughter: Okay. Like what?

Mom: Well, when people ask you where you got that red hair, you could say your grandma was from Ireland, and that's where your hair came from. All the way from Ireland! Can you think of something else you could say?

Daughter: How about saying it's from all the carrots I eat?

Mom: That would be great, too!

Helping children become more comfortable talking with people slowly draws them into relationships that they may not have been willing to attempt before. Relationship-building takes time and practice, though, and parents may have to push their children a bit by arranging play dates and other activities that pull their kids away from their stuff and into relationships with others.

Show Your Love for People, Not Just for Stuff!

This card deals with the ability to express affection and interest in others, a vital social skill. Some children seem so strongly connected to their possessions that they lose sight of significant relationships. Their excessive interest in things, or stuff, can set the stage for a host of other problems, such as overreaction, sensitivity to "territory," and an avoidance of life priorities. Parents may feel pushed aside and even rejected by their child's narrow focus on things. However, these feelings of rejection will only compound the problem and increase the likelihood of family conflict.

You can use the **Show Your Love for People, Not Just for Stuff!** card to discuss your child's tendency to be overly focused on his or her stuff. Time your approach for when your child is acting particularly caring and loving. You might try saying that it's sometimes hard for you to see or hear your child's love when his or her head is stuck in a tunnel of stuff, or that it's hard for friends to fit into the tunnel. You also can broaden this metaphor to include such prompts as, "Is there any daylight in that tunnel of stuff for a mom to connect with her kid for a few minutes?"

Parents also want to pave the way for mutual respect and healthy give-and-take with their children by modeling good behavior when playing with their kids. You don't always have to do it the child's way—some parents are extremely deferential—and the point is to stretch the child's relationships with others. Take the opportunity to be in charge, take turns, share, talk about "my ideas and your ideas," and work to pave the way to stronger relationships with friends and family.

Chapter 9
DON'T TRUST YOUR JEALOUS FEELINGS!

Being around other kids, especially friends, brothers, and sisters, can trigger strong feelings of jealousy. Maybe you see what they have, or the way your parents treat them. Sometimes it seems like other kids have better things or are getting treated like they're superspecial. **Jealous feelings** can make you focus only on what you don't have. When jealously takes over, it's easy to forget all the neat stuff you do have and how much your parents do for you, too. When this happens, your reacting side may get you to strike out with angry words at a friend, brother, sister, or even a parent.

Before letting this happen, try reading this talk-to-yourself message:

I am feeling so jealous right now that I need my thinking side to kick into gear. I know it will help me control these strong feelings of **jealousy**. My thinking side will remind me about what's true, like how my parents really do love me, how I get plenty of stuff, and how it can't always be my turn to get what I want. I can tell my parents that **I'm feeling jealous** and ask for a hug to squeeze those feelings right out of me.

The Green-Eyed Monster

Jealousy is a strong emotion with which many children struggle in their daily lives. Jealousy can rear its ugly head when a friend gets a new skateboard or bike, when parents praise a sibling for an accomplishment, or when a fellow student receives an honor at school. Feelings of jealousy can leave children with a knot in their stomachs, anger at others, and a belief that the world is not fair. Jealousy can trigger a child's reacting side, damaging sibling and peer relationships and creating tension within families.

Feelings of jealousy often are associated with having younger siblings. Attitudes toward family life change and comparisons become common. Children keep careful watch of how parents treat them as compared to their siblings. They track what their siblings get in terms of attention and material goods, and younger siblings may pay particular attention to what their older siblings can do that they can't. Jealousy doesn't end with siblings, though. A child can be jealous of peers who might get something that the child really wants or who are able to do something that the child really wants to do.

Peer encounters can trigger these feelings of rivalry, which is at the root of most jealousy, but parents can help their children understand where these feelings of envy are coming from and how to use their thinking side to keep them under control.

Jealousy Leads to Unhappy Kids

Life is a challenge for children who are constantly beset with jealous feelings. Rather than look at themselves for who they are, what they have, and what they can do, they examine themselves through a looking glass of who others are, what others have, and what others can do. Leading their lives this way can leave these children with feelings of emptiness and longing. Jealous children usually diminish what they do have and elevate what they don't have, leaving themselves vulnerable to painful feelings of envy that keep them from enjoying the everyday things they have in their lives and from appreciating their own unique abilities and accomplishments.

Jealousy also limits kids in social and family interactions because it sometimes makes them avoid people and activities that cause such feelings. For example, a boy playing hockey with friends might get upset because others keep scoring on him. Rather than laugh with his friends, he'll grab all the equipment and leave the game. Children who experience jealousy of others are more prone to quit activities, such as organized sports, rather than face up to children who they perceive as better. They see themselves as diminished. Rather than just having fun playing the game and doing their best, they conduct inner comparisons that are a huge hindrance to their ability to join in the game and have fun. These children often have an unhelpful internal voice that tells them things like, "I stink," "I can't throw as well as everybody else does," or "They're all better than me"—self-criticism that actually makes the activity unpleasant. Therefore, success in sports or social encounters is often experienced as either a loss or a feeding of the self-esteem, depending on the outcome of the encounter.

Helping Kids Let Go of Jealous Feelings

Children in families with more than one child do a lot of comparing and tend to experience feelings of jealousy more often than only children. A child may feel that a parent is more committed to an older or younger sibling. Praise, toys, and attention are all symbols of the parents' love. As children grow, they are supposed to assimilate their parents' love and grow to understand that they are loved fully, regardless of who got what on any particular day. Material goods and the physicality of the parents' relationship to the child become less important as love is understood internally. Older children realize that younger children need more time and attention. Younger children realize that their older siblings can do more right now, but that they'll eventually catch up.

For children who struggle to grow out of jealous feelings, parents may have to intervene and help them learn how to control these feelings. Parents can use the **Don't Trust Your Jealous Feelings!** card to get kids tuned in to their jealous feelings and to reflect on how those feelings can block out everything else that is good. You can have a Chalk Talk and remember a good time spent with your child and use those memories to help your child access good and satisfying feelings. Parents have to help their child understand that each day doesn't start with a scoreboard that keeps track of who gets what—"What have you done for me today?"—and that family life cannot be scripted so that everything is always even. This would be an impossible standard for any family to meet. Rather, parents need to help their children see that needs change day to day; a sibling may get more help and attention one day, while another child may get special treatment the next day. Over time, it usually balances out.

Head Off Jealousy Early On

A healthy relationship with siblings begins early on and helps prevent jealous feelings from developing. An effective way to do this is to help the older child develop an older brother/older sister mentality. Instead of just being mother's helper, parents can educate their older child about what's going on with a sibling, help the older child understand the needs of the younger child, and enlist the child's help in caring for the younger child.

Avoiding some common mistakes also helps keep jealousy at bay. Resisting the temptation to compare their children is difficult for many parents, but it's important. Although the intent of comparison is to make a point or change a behavior, the result may actually drive a wedge between the two siblings. Instead of looking for differences, parents can look for those behaviors that bring their children closer together. These behaviors can include compliments, offers to help, and warm tones of voice. Once the parent identifies these "sibling bond makers," they can coach each child in how the child can help make his or her brother or sister feel more secure and wanted and less jealous. Have a Chalk Talk with your child about things to can say and how to act to make the sibling feel good and, in return, have a happier relationship.

Another common mistake parents make is not intervening when jealous behavior results in an argument or fight. Some parents have been schooled to "let the two of them work it out," as if the result will be satisfactory to both children. It won't be. The outcome of a fight more often serves the needs of the older child and places the young one in an overly subservient role. Parents should firmly intervene and consider the source of the behavior. For example, the older sister may feel she is being pushed away from helping a younger sibling and will push back herself. Parents can help make the child aware of what she is doing and why she is doing it. Parents also should come to fights with answers, not just questions. In their role as detectives, parents often come seeking the facts and wind up getting two completely different stories. Rather than focusing on conflicting accounts of what happened, the parent can offer individual answers to resolve the problem. For example, if the older sister repeatedly tries to "spoil" the fun of her younger brother, parents can coach her to not trust her jealous feelings. They can explain how jealous feelings originate and discuss ways to control those feelings.

Parents can also help their children handle jealousy by acknowledging that such feelings are normal and a fact of life. But, having the feelings and acting on them are two different things. Parents need to clarify for their children that they can be jealous, but they shouldn't let the jealousy isolate them socially, academically, and competitively. Parents need to instill in their children the values, priorities, and principles used to lead a fulfilling life and teach them that they must learn to accept that there will always be those who have more than they do, and there will always be those who have less.

Don't Trust Your Jealous Feelings!

Jealousy can make family and peer relationships tense, competitive, and emotionally charged. A child's reacting side may jump into action as she responds with anger to whatever is perceived as unfair, and parents may scramble to make decisions seem as fair as possible. Often, the problem is not rooted in parental favoritism but in children not understanding jealousy and how it gets expressed.

The capacity to withstand jealous feelings without acting on them taps into the emotional skill of tolerance. The **Don't Trust Your Jealous Feelings!** card shows how jealousy can cover up children's awareness of all the good things they actually do receive from family life and their peers. Talk about the card's illustration and ask your child how the girl in the picture might be feeling and what she can do about those feelings. Parents are encouraged to openly discuss with their child that jealousy is normal and expected, but it's also a feeling that a child's thinking side can learn to control.

Chapter 10
BE FLEXIBLE!

Most times in your life, you expect things to happen the way they happened before. For example, when you go to the movies you expect to get there on time, buy tickets, and enjoy watching the show. But things don't always work out. You might get there late or discover the tickets are sold out. This situation can make you feel very disappointed. Your reacting side may take control, making you feel this is the worst thing in the world. **It can be very hard to be flexible** when you feel this way. **Being flexible** means using your thinking side to handle disappointments so that you can feel better sooner.

Read this talk-to-yourself message to become more flexible:

I must accept that I don't have control over a lot of things in life. I'm going to be disappointed sometimes. I can prepare for this by telling myself to **be flexible**, especially when I'm really looking forward to something. When I do get disappointed, I can tell myself, "Maybe it will work out better for me next time." Even though I can't stop bad things from happening, I can stop myself from reacting so badly to them. **I can be flexible.**

Handling What the World Throws at Us

Every day, life throws twists and turns at our children. A planned outing to the park is canceled when a sibling becomes ill. The TV set has to go in for repairs and favorite shows are missed. The shirt she really, really wanted to wear to school is in the laundry. A toy he had saved his allowance for is sold out. So on and so on. In some children, such disappointments trigger their reacting side. They become frustrated and stubborn, seek to put blame somewhere, and adopt an end-of-the world attitude.

Maria was on a driving tour of three national parks with her family. Plans were made and changed, and daily frustrations were inevitable, all a normal part of a family road trip. Erin, Maria's nine-year-old daughter, was holding to the family plan of going to a particular hotel to see a show. But Maria could see it wasn't going to happen. It was a long walk to the hotel, everyone was hot and tired, and the family consensus was to bag it. But Erin did not want to give in. Erin was in a tunnel where her thinking side had shut down, and she wouldn't take anyone else's needs into consideration. Her ensuing bad mood at not getting her way put a damper on the day for everyone.

Growing Up Elastic

Flexibility is the ability to adapt to change, a vital skill for parents to communicate to their children. Children need to be prepared for whatever the environment throws at them. Much of this behavior is learned early in childhood. All kids have a wish for some degree of control over their environment. This degree varies from child to child and becomes more apparent as a child's personality develops. Parents can see early on that some children move easily from crib to bed and from high chair to booster seat, while other children protest mightily. A child with little flexibility may have a difficult time recovering from the disappearance of a favorite juice cup because such events infringe on the child's sense of control. As children grow, events remind them they aren't in control. For example, a preschooler may refuse to put art supplies back so others can use them, preferring to keep control and be the art supplies monitor. Such behavior is an early harbinger of inflexibility.

To some extent, flexibility and inflexibility are inborn and temperamentally based. But in certain circumstances, where parents are either particularly overindulgent or withholding, children may develop inflexible tendencies. Parents like this haven't found the right balance between frustration and satisfaction. They try to script family life so the child can't possibly be disappointed, and that gets in the way of building flexibility.

The **Be Flexible!** card helps parents begin a discussion about what it means to have an open or closed mind in life. A closed mind is only satisfied having what it wants when it wants it. An open mind accepts the possibility that there are other satisfactions. The **Be Flexible!** card will help your child use his or her thinking side to embrace the idea of being open to other options.

The Costs of Inflexibility

Inflexibility produces all sorts of problems in a child's life. For example, in school, much of the day is teacher-led, and children must conform to and accept the teacher's authority. A lack of flexibility leads to social, emotional, and academic consequences for a child when peers and teachers respond negatively to his or her inability to bend. Children, however, don't necessarily understand the negative consequences of their behavior. They are more apt to feel disliked and victimized and believe the whole world is against them. Their inflexibility colors other people's perceptions of them, often with far-reaching consequences. The inflexible child is seen as mean, selfish, and spoiled, when what it really boils down to is a simple lack of flexibility.

Inflexible kids suffer in other ways, too. They often develop rigid routines, and, if a teacher alters the routine, inflexible children are likely to resist. They often will overstep their boundaries to enforce rules for other children and even for their parents. For example, a mother may always bring a snack for the car ride home after school. If she forgets one day, the inflexible kid will become very upset and unwilling to listen to possible alternatives ("Maybe we can stop at the convenience store and pick up something?"). Such cases are particularly frustrating for parents who find it hard to be patient and understanding when a setback that seems minor triggers a major reaction.

Children who are easily disappointed because of their own inflexibility often seek to make others suffer as well. The child wants to make you feel as bad as he does, even if you have no control over the situation. A common scenario: There is a movie a child badly wants to see, but when the family gets to the theater, the movie is sold out. The parent offers another movie as an option, but the child can't recover from his disappointment and see that the alternative is almost as good. Instead, the child will spend the rest of the evening suffering and pouting—and making everyone else suffer, too.

When an inflexible child is looking forward to something, it is hard to understand when things don't go as planned. The child has a rigid view of what is supposed to happen and, in her mind, the will of the world is being violated. If the rule of constancy is violated and something that is supposed to happen doesn't, the child has a difficult time recovering.

Learning Flexibility

For children predisposed to inflexibility, learning to catch what life throws at them takes time and practice. The first thing parents can do is to prepare their child when they see a potential bump in the road heading the child's way. For example, if your child has been saving his or her allowance for weeks to buy a set of trading cards, prepare him or her for the possibility that the store may have sold out of those cards. Have a Chalk Talk with your child to discuss what might happen and what the child will do if the cards are sold out. Before even going, the child can call the store and find out if the cards are in stock. If the cards are sold out, the child can find out when more will be coming in or decide to spend the money on something else. Talking with your child about the possibility of disappointment leads to setting up an acceptable plan B.

For example, plan A might be to go to the movies to see the latest Nickelodeon feature. But, if that's sold out, plan B would be to go to another theater and see the new Disney feature. Making children aware of two plans helps them understand that, if the first one doesn't happen, there is a backup and they will still get to have fun.

The third part of helping children become more flexible is praising them when they do show that trait. A parent might say, "I was really proud of how you handled it when you found that the movie was sold out. I know you were really excited to see it, but you showed how flexible you can be, and that made going to the other movie lots of fun, too."

When children are disappointed, the thinking side is being tested, and sometimes it's tough to keep the reacting side under control. They lose the big picture and they want to blame somebody. It's as if they have a blindfold on to all the other good stuff and, instead, stay in an end-of-the-world mode. It may help if the parent talks about past experiences when their child did exhibit flexibility and how proud they were and prepare their child ahead of time for all possibilities, good and bad.

If something does go wrong, parents also need to give their kids a little latitude. Disappointment is to be expected, and most kids will express it as a normal discharge of their emotions. As long as the discharge is temporary and not physically aggressive or mean-spirited, parents should give their child a little clemency and not be overly punitive. An understanding of a child's disappointment is very helpful. That being said, if a child continues to stew in disappointment and it moves from an impulsive response to a purposeful, continuing behavior, a parent should not reward the child by trying to make everything better. If a child is on a misery mission—really trying to make you miserable—plan B should be stashed for another time. A child should have five or ten minutes to play out disappointment, and then the parent should expect the child to regroup.

Having to deal with disappointments is simply a part of life, but parents can help their children see such times as character-building and can help them develop their flexibility. By looking for success, children see that sometimes they are able to handle disappointments, and when they do, things go better for everyone.

Be Flexible!

Erin, with the help of her mom, Maria, is working on becoming more flexible. Maria has used the **Be Flexible!** card to help Erin reduce her struggles with disappointments from one or two hours to a few minutes. Maria said Erin is now better able to work through a disappointment, get over it, and move on. Erin is, Maria says, developing an attitude that sometimes she has to be flexible with what happens, because she can't change it or blame anybody.

The **Be Flexible!** card is designed to help children avoid negative outbursts by becoming flexible. The more flexible your child is, the more easily he or she will be able to take things in stride. Children who can adapt to changing circumstances are happier, more emotionally secure in a variety of settings, and better able to pursue goals in the face of unexpected obstacles.

Use this card to teach your children to avoid becoming negative when events don't go their way. Read the card together, especially the talk-to-yourself message, "Maybe it will work out better for me next time." When a disappointing situation is before them, rather than trying to talk them out of seeing things as unfair, gently make them aware that the situation requires flexibility. Express empathy ("I understand that this is disappointing"); give your child time to discharge feelings appropriately; and guide your child to acceptance ("We can't change what happened, but we can make the most of what we have now"). It's especially important to point out success in being flexible in the face of disappointment. Many children do not know when they are managing a situation well, since this response doesn't trigger the intense feelings that often mark important experiences in their memories. Saying, "Now that was being flexible," provides an emphasis to their positive behavior that they might otherwise overlook.

Chapter 11
COOPERATION!

it can be very hard to cooperate when you just don't want to. Your parents (or teachers) may ask you to do something when all you want is for them to leave you alone!

Next time this happens, read this talk-to-yourself message:

Being cooperative is an important part of growing up. Even though it may feel like they're too bossy, my parents and teachers are really trying to help me become more responsible. If I learn how to **be cooperative**, then people will be more likely to **cooperate** with me when I ask them to do stuff. I'll also find that once I simply do what they ask, I'll feel better about myself. Plus, they'll be proud to see that I was able to **cooperate** even when I didn't want to.

Your reacting side makes you feel as if **cooperating** is giving up and caving in. It isn't. **Cooperating** is about letting your thinking side take charge of your behavior. Deep down inside, you know that life goes much more smoothly when you cooperate. And remember: **C.T.F.T. (Cooperate the First Time).** Doing this will lead to the good results that make **cooperating** worth the effort.

Cooperation: Learning How to Help Out

When Susan is out with her nine-year-old son Chris, she likes to point out people cooperating. At traffic lights, in grocery lines, at the post office, she makes sure Chris understands how people cooperate with each other so that the world works. On the family's dining room table, the Parent Coaching Cards sit in a bowl, available for spontaneous discussion, and it's often the **Cooperation!** card that sparks interest.

Susan says that Chris is learning that cooperation in the little things, like taking out the trash or feeding the family pet, helps him get ready for cooperation in the big things, like school, work, and the social world around him. Understanding the role cooperation plays in life at home and in the community, Susan says, is incredibly meaningful. Chris is learning the all-important lesson that if he wants people to cooperate with him when he needs something, he must cooperate with his mom, dad, friend, or teachers when they ask something of him.

Cooperation is mostly a learned skill. Though a child's temperament accounts for some of his willingness to cooperate, parents must set themselves up early on as role models and provide their child with a clear set of expectations when it comes to cooperating.

Early in a child's life, the parent is the sole measuring stick of cooperation. A baby's behavior may evoke praise, a soothing smile, or a comforting touch. Other behaviors may garner a disapproving glance and a sterner voice. The child watches a parent's response carefully and typically works hard to get positive responses. As a child approaches toddlerhood, there is a greater desire for autonomy, and the child works to differentiate herself from the parent. Some of this desired autonomy takes the form of uncooperativeness. The child learns to push the parents' buttons and gets pleasure from watching how they react. The more parents react, the more power that child has. Understanding cooperation at this age is still difficult, because the child has a hard time seeing the benefits, and parents need to focus on communicating and teaching their child to understand the rules and customs of the house.

When a child heads off to school, he is typically more cooperative than at home because of group pressure, regimentation, and strong modeling. Also, the emotional tag on the teacher is not nearly as strong as that with the parent. But back at home, with less routine and order than school, the child may fall back on pushing parental buttons by not cooperating.

How Parents Can Cultivate Cooperation

Looking at the **Cooperation!** Parent Coaching Card, you can see that this boy is smiling—and not because he is having fun. Taking out the trash isn't something he really wants to do, but he will do it to please his parents and feel better about himself. The smile and thumbs-up come from making a parent happy through cooperative behavior. But how do parents move from a grumpy "I don't want to," when a child is asked to take the trash out, to an "OK, Dad!"?

Parents can cultivate in their child a cooperative attitude that is rooted in approval-seeking. Kids can be very industrious and want to produce and please, but they may need help in developing an inventory in their minds that they can be proud of and draw from when they are asked to cooperate again. Parents can help children do this by telling them how much they appreciate their help when they set the table without even being asked. They can tell their children how proud they were of them when they took the dog out for a walk, even though the weather wasn't that great. "The way you watered the garden today really helped me out, and I appreciate what you did"—positive comments like this made to your child, either alone or in front of another grown-up, can help the child feel proud about what he or she did and more eager to help out the next time.

There also are social payoffs to cooperation many children aren't even aware of, and it's important for parents to gently point these out. Have a Chalk Talk with your child about how other people notice a child's inventory of skills and take note of whether a child is cooperative or not. Children who are not cooperative sometimes suffer great social costs. They may not be invited to a birthday party or over to a friend's house to play, because the parent or friend does not want to be around an uncooperative child. And at home, the uncooperative child invites nagging, stress, and punishment from her parents—all behaviors that diminish the quality of family life.

Another tool parents can use is to point out cooperative behavior when they see it in others and then discuss it with their children. For example, at the park a mother may ask her daughter to check on her baby brother. The Chalk Talk between the watching parent and child may go something like this:

> **Mother:** That little girl looked like she was having fun with her friends. I bet she didn't really want to go check on her baby brother.
>
> **Daughter:** No, I bet she didn't.
>
> **Mother:** Why do you think she did?
>
> **Daughter:** I don't know; maybe she was worried about him.
>
> **Mother:** Maybe, too, she realized it wouldn't take very long and this was a chance to show she could cooperate and make her mom proud of her.

To help children understand the sometimes-abstract notion of cooperation, parents also can Chalk Talk the idea of having a "Mr. or Miss Opposite" part of their personalities. You might say to your daughter, for example, "Miss Opposite is no friend of yours. She tries to get you to do the opposite of what you're supposed to do, and that leads to trouble. Look out, because you never know when Miss Opposite will pop up."

Parents can help their children see that mom and dad are not trying to be mean and boss them around, but are trying to help their children grow and understand that better things will happen for them when they cooperate. Cooperation can lead to better friends, special treats, and a love inside that gets prouder and prouder.

Bribery as a Means to Cooperation

Too many parents resort to bribery as a way to coerce their children into cooperation. Kids pick up on this game pretty quick, and it can rapidly spiral out of control. For example, a parent at a grocery store may tell a crying child, "If you be quiet and behave, I'll get you a candy bar when we leave." This gets away from developing cooperation as a character trait and moves toward coercing cooperation with the promise of an external reward. Parents should, instead, set expectations with a Chalk Talk that puts boundaries on behavior. You might say, for example, "When we go to the grocery store, it is not to buy candy. I don't want to hear any 'Can I haves.' If you can't cooperate, there will be consequences."

The parent needs to set the stage so that he or she is not rewarding cooperation but, rather, expecting it as standard behavior. To do this, parameters have to be set on behavior, and children have to clearly understand what those parameters are. Is there any room for rewards? Absolutely. A formalized weekly allowance system allows a parent to recognize their child's cooperation in doing chores without tying a reward to any one activity.

Cooperation in the Middle School Child

Cooperation skills often seem to flag in the middle school child. Kids are developing independent notions of the world, are more socially influenced, and feel their parents need to be seen and not heard. At this age, parents should be more sensitive to children's egos, ease of embarrassment, and developing attitudes. Their abilities to cooperate should be considered in light of this phase in their of development. But parents shouldn't give up and tolerate a totally errant child. Instead, recognize that your child may not be as cooperative as he or she once was for many reasons, some of which are beyond the child's own sphere of control. Children are strongly influenced by outside forces—peers; new technology, like instant messaging; and media role models—that may help to shape a less-than-cooperative personality. Early on, parents can help their children through this stage by recognizing and explaining these forces to their children and showing them how strongly they can be influenced by them. Open communication may not cure everything, but it goes a long way to stemming problems that, left on their own, can spiral out of control.

Preventing the Obligatory Battle

Most parents and children have experienced the contests of will that uncooperative behavior often leads to. Most parents are veterans of these so-called "cooperation battles." It starts out with a simple, "Would you please set the table?" then, "I asked you to set the table," then, "Set the table now!" A good approach to take with your child is to have a sit-down Chalk Talk about unnecessary battles. You might say to your child, for example, "I feel like we are heading for a battle over cooperation, and it is so unnecessary. Instead of both of us getting angry, me feeling worn out, and you eventually doing what I asked you to do anyway, why don't you just do what I ask the first time I ask, and then we can avoid all of this?" This sort of conversation appeals to the child's sense of responsibility while, at the same time, it reinforces the parent's message that he or she can see the coming struggle and would rather that everyone not have to go through it.

Reciprocity of Life

There are very few people in this world who are truly altruistic, but many parents expect their children to be just that. A better approach may be to explain to children that, if they do for others without complaint, others will be happy to do for them. Cooperating sends a message to the world about how giving and unselfish a person is and how the person is able to put the needs of others ahead of his or her own. Reciprocity kicks in when we need something, and people are more apt to cooperate when we cooperate with them and help out when needed.

Cooperation!

Uncooperative behavior is a common problem and one that has a negative impact on a child's relationships. Children who have a difficult time cooperating tend to view it narrowly as submitting to parental authority. By pairing cooperation with maturity, you can refocus your child on the bigger picture: "It's not about giving in, it's about growing up." The **Cooperation!** Parent Coaching Card reinforces the notion that cooperative children tend to receive more privileges because parents (and other adults) can trust them to follow the rules. And, because peers admire them, they are also offered more opportunities for new and different kinds of fun. Cooperative kids are nicer to be around, and other kids like to be with kids who can cooperate.

Parents may want to stress to their child that "cooperation counts" in the minds of other children, since friendship tends to be measured, in part, by this critical social skill. Children who are obstinate and stubborn, who refuse to cooperate in sports, games, and friendship activities, may find themselves wondering why they don't get invited to birthday parties and play dates anymore. It's up to parents to help the child see that cooperation is key to peaceful family relationships and happy friendships. Help your child to CTFT—Cooperate the First Time!

Chapter 12
SAY IT AND SHOW IT WHEN YOU GET IT!

People probably do nice things for you—buying stuff, driving you places, or just doing you a favor. Problems can occur when you act like you expect nice things from others. You may forget to say "thank you" and **show that you mean it**. Or, you may react like you want something bigger and better. If you do that, people will become angry and you'll end up getting less of what you really want.

Your thinking side can help you remember to say "thank you" and show that you mean it, even if you don't like something all that much.

Read this talk-to-yourself message to learn how:

Sometimes I get what I want and sometimes I get what I don't really want. Either way, somebody is taking the time to do something for me. Even if I don't like something, I should try to remember that the other person wasn't trying to disappoint me. An important part of growing up is **being considerate** of others' feelings. This means saying and **showing that I appreciate the efforts people put into trying to make me happy**.

What Do You Say?

Today's parents often feel unappreciated by their children. They feel that they give, give, give, and the kids take, take, take with little appreciation of what is being done for them or given to them. Or, a child at a birthday party rips through presents and doesn't even pause to express appreciation for gifts given by friends and relations, while the parent chimes in hopefully, "What do you say?" Or, even worse, the child makes comments about "already having that," "not liking that," or showing with body language extreme disappointment in a gift—much to a parent's chagrin and embarrassment.

Good manners are important skills children develop over time by watching adults and other children, discussing what is expected in social and family situations, and learning from their mistakes. The ability to show appreciation in a sincere and timely manner is one such skill. But too many parents mistakenly believe that children instinctively know how to show appreciation. As with many other social skills, a sense of appreciation develops over time and is fostered by the modeling behavior of parents. The **Say It and Show It When You Get It!** Coaching Card helps children use their thinking sides to show appreciation, even when their reacting sides are not feeling very appreciative.

A sense of appreciation is especially important as the consumptive climate in our world makes some people perceive today's children as spoiled. Parents often remind children that when they were young, they received gifts only on birthdays, and Christmas or Hanukkah—and not lots of gifts, just a few things. Buying habits have changed, and children receive gifts and goods often and many times for no reason at all. Because of this, children can develop a sense of entitlement that creates in them expectations, and when thanks are not forthcoming from their children, parents can feel angry and unappreciated.

I Want!

In Roald Dahl's book *Charlie and the Chocolate Factory*, Veruca Salt is the spoiled child who gets everything she wants when she wants it. Her parents are trained to jump at her every scream. Veruca is the extreme version of a child who thinks only about her own needs and wants. But many children also struggle with their own desires. A facet of the **Say It and Show It When You Get It!** card is that sometimes it is not the child's turn to "get." For these children, it may be difficult to go to birthday parties where they won't be getting a gift or to be happy for a sibling who has just gotten a new toy.

Using the **Say It and Show It When You Get It!** card, parents can explain that it is not always the child's turn and that life is full of turn-taking—sometimes someone else gets to have special fun and get special gifts. Children can think back on special times they had or gifts they received to remind themselves that they get turns, too.

Teach Your Children Appreciation

You can help your children learn how to show appreciation by practicing with some Chalk Talks. For example, before your child's birthday party, you may want to take him or her aside and explain that you expect the child to show appreciation for his or her gifts.

Mother: At your birthday party today, I want you to remember to thank each person as you open your gifts. I'd like for you to make a nice comment like, "This is really cool," to show your appreciation.

Daughter: But what if I don't like it?

Mother: You have to remember that you may not get exactly what you want, but that someone worked hard to do something nice for you, and you should appreciate that.

Daughter: But what if I already have the same thing?

Mother: That doesn't really change what I said. That person didn't intend to buy you the same thing and was trying to do something really nice. You can just say "thank you" and make a nice comment.

Daughter: But I don't want to have two of the same thing.

Mother: After the party, we can talk about exchanging the gift. But at your party, when you open the present, that's not the time to do that. Can you think of something you might say if you *do* get a toy you already have?

Daughter: Maybe I could say, "Thanks, I really like this."

Mother: I think that would be great and make the other person feel good.

Another important concept for children to understand is that when they show appreciation for the things people do for them, people are more likely to do things for them in the future. Just as children want their efforts to be noticed and appreciated, they should understand that other children and adults want to feel like what they have done is important.

The best way to teach appreciation, however, is to model it at home and in social settings for your children. When over at a friend's house for dinner, express to the hostess how much you appreciate the wonderful meal and how much work must have gone into the preparations. When children hear their parents expressing appreciation for what someone else has done for them, they quickly learn that good manners matter. Use the **Say It and Show It When You Get It!** card to start a conversation with your child about the importance of good manners and about how being considerate of other people's feelings shows that he or she is growing up.

Say It and Show It When You Get It!

How many times have you said, "What do you say?" after your child has received something? "Oh yeah, thank you," answers your child, while you wonder if he or she will ever remember to spontaneously express appreciation.

Children learn social skills through observation, experience, and reflection, not because parents prompt them to say and do things at the right time. Prompting them to provide the "right answers" tends to foster your child's dependence on you for on-the-spot social skills assistance. Chalk Talk the manners on the **Say It and Show It When You Get It!** card before a social encounter in which a child is likely to receive a gift or special gesture. Stress that one of the true tests of "being older" (or "mature," depending on your child's age) is the ability to express appreciation and caring. Saying and showing "thank you" is a caring behavior other people notice.

Chapter 13
BEAT THE FEAR!

Fear can creep up on you anytime, anyplace, and about anything. Maybe you **feel scared** as you walk onto the bus, sit in class, or attend some type of practice. **Fear attacks** your body and your mind. Your body feels all wobbly and your thoughts seem to turn against you. You become so worried about something bad happening that you do not deal so well with what is really going on. You end up believing that your **fear** came true—but it didn't. What really happened is that you fell into **the fear trap**.

The next time you start feeling scared, read this talk-to-yourself message:

I am not going to let **fear** control my reactions anymore. Avoiding things that other kids enjoy because I'm afraid means less fun for me. I deserve fun and freedom, too. My thinking side can help me plan ahead to deal with scary things. Things won't always work out the way I want. But when they don't, I'll know **fear** didn't stop me from trying. I am going to use all my courage and determination to **beat the fear** when I feel it creeping up on me.

Ryan's Story

When Ryan was two and a half years old, he had a near-drowning experience that set him up for a seemingly unbeatable fear of water. Through the years, Ryan clung to his mother, Anna, in the pool. While his friends were jumping off the diving board, playing Marco Polo in the deep end, or racing the length of the pool, Ryan stayed with his mom in the shallow end. At first, Anna thought they could beat Ryan's fear by talking about it, by taking more swimming lessons, or by just letting him be in the shallow water where he felt comfortable.

As Ryan approached adolescense, it became apparent that this approach was not working. Anna was at a loss as to what to do and became increasingly frustrated by her son's unwavering anxiety. Ryan's fear was also affecting his comfort with his friends and his ability to engage in social activities. It was during this time that Anna was introduced to the Parent Coaching Cards. Flipping through them, Anna was instantly drawn to the card with the picture of a boy at a swimming pool. It was, she says, Ryan.

Ryan began using the **Beat the Fear!** card to give himself the self-talk he needed to overcome his fear and let his thinking side take over for his reacting side. Anna relates how Ryan would "talk himself up" before his swim lesson, telling himself he would not let his fear keep him from having fun. Over time, the words held more and more meaning for Ryan, and his fear did not keep him from having fun. Today, Anna says, Ryan swims like a fish, and anytime he faces a situation that makes him apprehensive, he repeats his mantra: "I deserve to have fun!"

Understanding Fear

The roots of fear begin to grow early in a child's life, when the child first begins to separate good from bad. In a newborn, comfort, feeding, and cuddling resonate as good things. Hunger, stomach stress, and physical pain become preverbal memories of bad things. Emotions such as fear begin to develop, too. The startle reflex is one of the early physical foundations of fear. Stranger anxiety is another form of fear that kicks in at around the age of nine months. Fear begins in a child's early experiences and grows as the child grows in awareness of the world around him or her.

Fear takes on a physical nature as a child progresses into toddlerhood. Distance from a parent or the inability to find a parent registers in the body as a feeling of tightness and can set off feelings of panic. Almost everyone has seen a child crying inconsolably when accidentally separated from his parent at the store, if only for a minute. Such intense physical feelings give fear even more potency.

As children continue to progress socially, the list of situations that can strike fear in their hearts grows, too. Day care, school, birthday parties, and activities away from their parents can all be fearful experiences for children. A child's own experience also figures greatly into what fears she harbors. If the child was bitten by a dog, slipped in the shower, or fell down the stairs, similar situations can trigger fear if and when they arise. A child may become afraid of all dogs, unwilling to take a shower, or timorous around stairs.

Situational fear and early traumatic experiences are two factors in creating a child's personal fear index. A third factor is a child's own temperament. Children come into the world with distinct personality traits that enable some to be fearless (even to the point of creating fear in their parents) and others to be fearful of ordinary things, like trucks driving by, birds flying overhead, or insects crawling underfoot. Going hand in hand with temperament are a child's limitations—perceived or real—as well as his or her physical abilities. Children who are fearful of water may simply not have adequate swimming skills. As they become older, more is expected of them—like jumping off the diving board into the deep end—and they become even more fearful.

A parent also must be on the lookout for a child's hidden fears, those fears created by situations or events that the parent may not be aware of. Children often develop rituals to avoid the things they are afraid of, without a parent even being aware that a fear exists. For example, a child may be afraid of riding his bike up a driveway incline and may always dismount on the approach. Or, a child may avoid a certain piece of playground equipment, never venturing near the merry-go-round or the tube slide. All of these fears, while small, can become controlling and teach the child that the best way to deal with fear is to avoid fearful situations, creating even more paralyzing behavior.

The Cost of Fear

Fear that keeps a child out of dangerous situations is important. But fear that has no reality base only serves to limit a child from taking all that life has to offer. Fear can impose many restrictions and constrictions that can carry into adulthood by negatively affecting choices and by feeding fear barriers. For example, if a child is afraid of joining organized activities, this plants the seeds for her social interactions as she grows older. As a teen, she may be afraid to attend dances. As a college student, she may look with trepidation at the notion of meeting new people. As an adult, she may isolate herself from unfamiliar social situations and shy away from new relationships or important challenges. The longer the seed of fear remains planted, the more time it has to grow.

Helping Your Child Overcome the Fear Obstacle

For Ryan, fear of water was a huge obstacle physically, emotionally, and mentally. He could see how his fear was keeping him from having fun. His mother was concerned that not only was Ryan's fear holding him back socially, but he also was not a "water-safe" kid. If ever he did get in water over his head, with no lifeguards or parents around to rescue him, he would be in grave danger. That was one handicap she did not want him to have.

Parents can help their children overcome their fears, but it is usually a gentle, one-step-at-a-time approach. Threats aren't effective (and can be downright cruel), and a sink-or-swim attitude usually only creates more fear in the child. Parents also need to be aware of how mothers and fathers oftentimes differ in their treatment of a fearful child. Fathers have a tendency to demand more, without providing supportive coaching—"Come on now, all the other kids can do it." For example, some children find learning to ride a bicycle without training wheels to be a long and difficult process. The wheels come off, the child falls, and the child immediately wants the wheels back on again. Some parents, fathers in particular, simply refuse to put the wheels back on and thus create even greater fear in their children. A better approach is to support the child and offer to put the wheels back on after the child has had a few days to recover. Giving the child time may give him or her the courage to try again. The key is to support the child no matter where the child is in facing his or her fears. Support should not be conditional on the child's success in overcoming fear.

Using the Parent Coaching Card

Some children limit activities and avoid opportunities because they fear injury, failure, rejection, or the unknown. Parents can become frustrated, worried, and confused about how to help their children. They wonder if they should push or just let the child deal with the situation in his or her own way. But facing a "fear challenge" often requires more emotional skills than the child has, and the child needs his parents to help gain those skills and face his fears.

The **Beat the Fear!** Coaching Card focuses on helping a child's thinking side take control to push out fear. Parents can discuss the card before the child is faced with what parents know will be a fearful situation. For example, Angela may want to ride a roller coaster with her friends at the amusement park, but her fear is keeping her feet solidly on the ground. Before heading off to the amusement park, Angela's father may Chalk Talk about the fear trap and how fear is keeping Angela from having the fun she deserves to have. Angela's father can relate his own experience about overcoming fear and having fun on the rides and talk about the safety of the rides. Angela can practice the talk-to-yourself message to beat the fear when it starts creeping up on her.

Parents also can pull in other **Beat the Fear!** ambassadors to help incorporate the card's message into the child's daily life. By educating others about the card—the language, catch phrases, and goals—parents can enlist the aid of teachers, coaches, other parents, and instructors to complement the parent's efforts with the child. In this manner, the parent is not the sole supplier of coaching wisdom and guidance. The effect of having more than one coaching adult multiplies the child's ability to tackle his or her fears.

Turn Fear Around

The two main emotional skills required to conquer fear are courage and determination—courage to face the fear and determination to overcome it. When facing a fear, parents should not support their child's avoidance of the thing or activity that is feared. If the fear is a result of an event that was sudden and traumatic, like a dog bite, the child will need time to recover but then can be gently reintroduced to dogs. This exposure may simply start with reading the child a book about dogs, looking at pictures of dogs, and then watching from inside the house as a dog walks by on the sidewalk. Such distant exposure helps the child develop an appreciation that all dogs are different. When the child is outside playing, a dog on a leash may walk by at a safe distance and help the child realize that one specific dog bit him and that not all dogs are like that.

When the child is comfortable with these small steps, the parent may select a very safe dog for their child to pet. Playing fetch and other games helps the child feel more in control of the dog and see the dog as a playmate, rather than something to be feared. Of course, parents will also want to teach their child how to be safe around dogs and all animals.

Reintroducing children to something they fear may take days, weeks, or even months. If a parent thinks of these steps as "fear stairs," they will realize that they can't push their child up the steps. The child may climb quickly, pause along the way to rest, or take each step slowly and deliberately. Some children make it halfway up and then clamor back down to the first step. Too many times parents misconstrue this as a failure, but it's important to reassure the child and let the child know it's OK to take a few steps back. Parents need to help their children understand that the capacity to will oneself up the fear stairs by calling up courage and determination is at the heart of overcoming fear. The goal of reaching the top of the stairs is not as important as the process of getting there, and the important skills children learn along the way will be ones they call upon often.

Each child is different in his or her ability to recover and move on from a traumatic event. But parents should not reinforce harbored fears and allow them to grow. Taking a child's fears seriously and helping the child deal with and conquer their fears can keep fear from becoming crippling.

Creative Approaches Help Kids Beat the Fear

Parents need to be very creative when devising techniques to help their child overcome fear. Encouraging a child to play with other children at the playground may take the form of the child singing "Make New Friends," giving voice to the child's courage. Making eye contact with adults can be a scary thing. A parent can play a game with a child to have the child see what eye color a person has or if the person wears contact lenses. Parents can also help their children become empowered by talking about their own fears and how they face them. Bringing fear out into the open can help children take back control.

For children who are afraid of going to bed at night, parents may practice positive imagery. For example, the child may picture that the bedroom door leads to a room that is a creation of the child's choosing, say, a place where it rains chocolates, a ballroom full of beautifully dressed dancers, or a room filled with snow for sledding. Parents can also plant with their children the idea of a "worry eraser." A child can visualize his or her fears on a chalkboard, erase them away, and replace them with positive images. Chalk Talks are another powerful tool. For example, many children are afraid of making phone calls, and parents can use a Chalk Talk like the following to help their child become more comfortable:

> **Mom:** I know you really want to have Colin come over, but I'd like it if you could make that phone call and invite him. Why don't we practice what you might say?

> **Son:** OK.

Mom: All right, I'll be Colin. The phone rings and Colin's dad answers. You might start by saying, "Hi, this is Danny. May I speak with Colin please?"

Son: OK. "Hi, this is Danny. May I speak with Colin?"

Mom: "Sure. Let me get him. . . . Hi, Danny."

Son: "Hi, Colin. Would you like to come over to my house to play tomorrow?"

Mom: "Sure, but let me check with my dad first. Hold on a sec. . . . Dad says that's fine. What time should he drop me off?"

Son: "How about one o'clock?'

Mom: "That sounds great. I'll see you tomorrow."

Son: "OK, bye."

Mom: That was great. Do you want to try it for real now?

Son: OK, but can you dial the phone for me?

Role-playing helps build confidence in children by giving them a predictor of what's going to happen. Practicing a phone call, giving a presentation to a parent before a child has to speak in class, and talking to an unfamiliar adult, all help children overcome their initial fear and see the situation for what it really is, not for the fearful thing they have built up in their minds.

Beat the Fear!

Some children limit activities and avoid opportunities because they fear injury, failure, rejection, or some other negative outcome. Sometimes avoidance is due to a fear of the unknown. Parents can become frustrated, worried, and confused about how to help and may wonder whether or not they should push.

Contending with fear requires the emotional skills of courage and determination. The **Beat the Fear!** card will help you direct your child's thinking away from the feared object and onto the fear itself. It can be helpful to remind your child of a time when the child successfully overcame a fear and how life improved as a result. Similarly, parents can explain how the image of the swimming pool on the illustration can be replaced by another situation their child can relate to, like calling a friend or performing at a recital. Learning to beat the fear is a lifelong skill that can help your child lead a more pleasurable, less stressful life.

Chapter 14
KNOW WHEN TO BACK OFF!

Being with others sometimes triggers problem behaviors. This can happen at home, school, at a friend's house, around the neighborhood, or just about anywhere. Usually the trigger is something you see or hear, involving the people you're with. Maybe they're upset at someone, are trying to have a private conversation, or have asked you to **butt out**. It can be very hard to do this when you want to be part of what's happening. Maybe you think you have the right solution. Maybe you just want to make yourself feel good or for them to feel bad. You will need to **"back off"** so they can deal with the situation.

Stop yourself from interfering and getting into trouble by reading this talk-to-yourself message:

Knowing when to **back off** will help keep me out of trouble. People don't want me **butting in** when they're trying to deal with something that doesn't involve me. If I interfere, I may become the next target! I can tell myself, "This doesn't involve me and I need to **back off** so that it doesn't become my problem, too." People will like and respect me more when I do this.

The Intrusive Child

Some children have a difficult time understanding when to get involved and when to back off. This usually derives from a sense of ownership that begins early in a child's life. As toddlers, these children may develop overly powerful attachments to things and people. If someone takes a toy away, they respond aggressively and forcefully. Their temperament often reflects an intense investment in people and things and a difficulty in respecting the boundaries of others. These children can be voracious in their desire to be included, to know what's going on, and to give their opinions and input. They intrude frequently into the "space" of others, yet they are often the children who have the most trouble handling it when others intrude into their space.

These children are often strongly possessive of their parents' time and attention and may have an out-of-proportion sense of entitlement. They view themselves as being at the center of their parents' interpersonal world. Parents drop everything to respond to the child, and the child eventually develops the sense that there are no limits. Interrupting conversations with "What are you talking about?" becomes second nature. When these children are young, such indulgences don't have too great of a social cost. But when they are older, not understanding their boundaries or respecting the space of others begins to have a cost. An older child is held more accountable for his or her behavior.

When Pam, age 14, began using the Parent Coaching Cards several years ago, one issue she struggled with was learning how to back off. She had a bad habit, she says, of always interrupting people, and she would get angry when people didn't respond well to what she had to say. Pam didn't even realize she was interrupting so much until her parents brought it to her attention. Using the **Know When to Back Off!** card, Pam began to recognize the signs of her intrusive behavior and worked hard to control her impulses. Over time, she says, she learned that she would get a better response from her parents, teachers, and friends if she paid attention to the environment around her, timed her comments better, and didn't interrupt conversations that didn't involve her. Breaking old habits was hard, Pam says, but the **Know When to Back Off!** card helped reinforce the positive changes she was making by reminding her not to let her reacting side take the controls away from her thinking side.

Parents and teachers regularly come into contact with children like Pam who love to participate and can't tolerate the thought of being left out of anything. They often overlook timing, boundaries, and reciprocity, so that instead of receiving the approval they crave, they feel unfairly treated and frustrated.

The World Is Such a Confusing Place

Understanding the nuances of the social world is a skill that takes time and practice. While some children seem more tuned in to the feelings and conditions of those around them, others struggle with the concept of space and their place in it. For example, a coach may be giving instructions, and the child who has difficulty understanding boundaries may chime in inappropriately with his own comments. Or a teacher may be calling a rule breaker to task, and the boundary-challenged child may pipe up with her take on the situation. Children usually don't do these things to be malicious—they think they are helping—but they end up crossing a boundary into someone else's territory.

Chalk Talk with your children some specific examples of social situations to better prepare them for what they might face in settings with their peers and other adults. Possible scenarios include: (1) when a parent is talking to a sibling, the child has the urge to jump into the driver's seat and take over the role of authority; (2) the child has gone over to a friend's house, and the friend has gotten a new skateboard, so the child jumps right into the role of teacher without being asked and takes the skateboard to show a few new tricks; (3) an older child takes over the play of a group of younger children without being asked; or (4) the parents are having a private conversation and the child becomes curious and interrupts, feeling like he or she has something to offer or needs to know what's going on. Egocentric thinking in many of these situations prompts the child to overstep boundaries.

Parents need to help their child understand that there is an invisible line that separates the child from others. Starting with the **Know When to Back Off!** card, children can use their thinking sides to learn to ask themselves, "Where should I be in relation to others? Should I be in their face coaching them when they haven't asked for my help?" It's helpful for your child to learn the notion of "clues" in the environment—who is there, how well the child knows the person, is the person involved in a conversation with someone else—so the child can give instructions to himself or herself on what to do. Letting the reacting side take over for the thinking side can make people angry with the child.

Talk with your child about how hard it is to resist overstepping boundaries. And let the child know that even though the child thinks he or she is trying to help, the child might end up getting hurt feelings or yelled at because he or she disregarded boundaries.

Parents can reinforce this message by pointing out a time when the child got boundaries right and respected the space of others. For example, a parent might say, "When I was talking with your sister, you really kept quiet. You knew your sister was feeling sensitive, and I could tell you knew when to back off. I'm proud of the way you kept your thinking side in charge and paid attention to the feelings of others." Parents can help their children understand that sometimes keeping quiet and being sensitive to the needs of others pays off more than butting in, and that other people will notice and appreciate their efforts. Parents need to note and verbally reward "backing-off" behavior when they see their children doing it right, as this social skill takes a lot of practice, and sometimes children don't even realize when they are doing it well.

Timing, Boundaries, and Reciprocity

A good analogy to use with your child to help him or her understand the **Know When to Back Off!** card is driving. Drivers have to learn to drive, share the road with others, and adjust for changing conditions—sometimes the road is smooth and sometimes it's bumpy. If a driver always tries to drive the same way without adjusting to the road and others around him or her, the driver will eventually make people mad or cause a crash. Likewise, children need to understand that there are rules for the road they are on, and those rules can change depending on conditions. Have a Chalk Talk with your child about the rules of the social road, including timing, boundaries, and reciprocity.

Timing

Timing is all about picking the right time to speak up so that what you have to say will be received in the best way possible. Have your child check these conditions to improve his or her timing: What's going on around the person? Is the person in the middle of a conversation with someone else? Is the person reading? What does the person's body language tell me? How important is it that I talk to the person right now? Is there something else more important that just happened? Can I wait to talk to the person another time? With practice, assessing social situations will become easier as your child becomes more attuned to the surrounding environment.

Boundaries

Boundaries are about the space that separates people from each other. If we are driving, it means keeping in our lane and not following too closely. For children, it means not invading the space of others but, instead, respecting their boundaries. Here are some things children can tell themselves to improve their handling of boundaries: "I need to notice the distance that separates other people when they are talking to each other. It's okay to ask people if they need time to themselves. I don't need to take it personally if someone does need more space. I need to remember that just because I like having people close and not putting up boundaries, not everyone feels the same way."

Reciprocity

Reciprocity has to do with thinking about the feelings of others before saying or doing something. If we are driving, it means being courteous, using turn signals, or letting drivers pass us. For kids, reciprocity is about sharing control over decision making, inviting others to express ideas, and asking the right kinds of questions. Kids can become more aware of reciprocity by asking themselves: "Is the other person as involved as I am? If not, I can try talking a little less and asking the person questions about his or her life." Encourage your child to also review the time spent with friends. Have the child think about how decisions were made and whether everybody got to have an equal hand in the outcome.

Know When to Back Off!

Opportunities abound for children to step into the problems and concerns of others. Some quickly "read" that certain situations do not warrant their involvement, while other children intrude without invitation, especially in emotionally charged circumstances. These intrusive children let their reacting sides take control and are drawn to, rather than repelled by, the emotional charge. Instead of realizing they are about to be blown up by an emotional land mine, they think they can restore calm and contribute to the well-being of others. Not surprisingly, conflict often results, and the offending child feels unfairly blamed for "just trying to help."

You can redefine "help" so that your child will eventually understand that helping includes using his or her thinking side to respect the boundaries of others. When your child is about to overstep boundaries, gently but firmly state to him or her, "Know when to back off," rather than, "Back off!" By stressing the concept "know when," you send an important message about social judgment without implying that your child is deliberately attempting to make things difficult for others. Refer to the illustration on this card, which shows a boy intruding into a girl's space and the negative reaction that this triggers. Chalk Talk with your child what the boy might be saying and how the girl is reacting to his intrusion. Have your child suggest how the boy might handle the situation differently, remembering the ideas of timing, boundaries, and reciprocity.

Chapter 15
STAY TUNED IN!

A lot goes on in your life every single day. You talk to many different people and spend time in several different places—at home, on the bus, in class, and at friends' houses. While you're at these places and talking with both kids and adults, people notice and listen to you. They notice what you talk about, whether you're listening, and how much you **pay attention to their feelings and ideas**.

You can show people that you are "**tuned in**" by carefully listening to what they say and keeping on the same track when it's your turn to talk. People will like you better when you remember to do this.

Read this talk-to-yourself message as a reminder to stay tuned in:

I will be better at making and keeping friends if I **stay tuned in**. This means not interrupting so much, not assuming others want to hear me talk a lot, and not bringing up something totally different from what's being discussed. **Staying tuned in** means I ask questions, mention things they have told me before, and show my interest by looking right at them.

It's All About Me

Children come into this world with big egos and strong needs. Parents enhance this egocentricity in the baby and young child by dispensing attention, responding rapidly to needs, and working hard to meet the demands of their child. But, over time, the child's egocentricity begins to diminish in the face of the desires and needs of others. The child goes through stages where the environment leads to the expectation of mutuality with other children and family members.

This first appears as parallel play, where the child is still greatly focused on his own needs but aware that someone else is in the room. Then, around the age of two or three, children begin mutual play, and their expectations begin to change. Other children and parents expect that the child will learn to share, take turns, put requests ("My toy!") into words rather than actions, and begin to be tuned in to those around him.

At preschool and in other social settings, "tuning in" is fostered through special activities, like circle time and show-and-tell, and by cooperating in class activities. As the child enters a formal school setting, expectations of tuning in and paying attention are even greater. The child is expected to raise his hand, listen to other children, answer questions, and be able to comment on what a teacher or another student is discussing.

This process can go awry in children for a number of different reasons. They may have trouble tuning in because of ADHD (attention deficit hyperactivity disorder), a temperament that makes it difficult for them to get and stay tuned in, parents who are overly permissive, or they may be developmentally lagging. Permissiveness may take the form of allowing a child to interrupt at any time, not listen if the child chooses not to, or hijack conversations with unrelated topics. This type of behavior perpetuates the belief in the child's mind that, if she has something to say, she can just go ahead and say it regardless of who is talking or what the topic of discussion is. These children often have a difficult time understanding the notion that they are just one member of a community, not the community itself.

Staying tuned in was especially a challenge for Jeremy, age nine, a child with ADHD who would often interrupt others, make comments not connected to the conversation, or simply drift away when someone was talking with him. His grandmother, Sandra, used the **Stay Tuned In!** card to help Jeremy understand the importance of listening in school, with his friends, and around his family members. She and Jeremy talked frequently about his thinking side and his reacting side, and she gave him insight about staying tuned in to what's going on around him and how this could help prevent the trouble that came from not listening.

The Art of Conversation

Parents are the first and best teachers of the art of conversation with their children. Their own ability to converse in a give-and-take manner models for their children what is desirable in their own conversations. Parents can also talk with their children about the importance of conversation in their lives and how tuning in helps them keep friends and gain the respect and appreciation of their teachers and parents.

The **Stay Tuned In!** card reflects this important social skill—a skill that comes naturally to some children but with great difficulty to others. Many parents are concerned because their children don't know how to keep conversations going with peers or adults and may sabotage conversations by making silly or unrelated comments, or they may seem simply unable to say anything at all. You can work with your child to help him or her develop a conversational style that is comfortable and to help your child get and stay tuned in.

Start with a commonsense template to guide your child's efforts. It's hard for children to understand the subtleties of social skills unless adults explain them in simple terms. Read and Chalk Talk the **Stay Tuned In!** card with your child. Here's how it might sound: "I've noticed that sometimes it's hard for you to get conversations going with other kids or that conversations go wrong. I can help with that. There are three things you can think about to help you get talk going with your friends and other people—greetings that go somewhere, common ground, and deeper discussion." For "greetings that go somewhere," you can compare knocking on the neighbor's door and saying "Hi," which doesn't get you anywhere, to saying, "Hi! How was practice yesterday?" which gets a conversation going. "Common ground" is where two people's interests overlap to provide a topic of conversation. Have your child look for clues to common ground, like soccer cleats or books, that can spark conversations. "Deeper discussion" is sharing one's own feelings or opinions about a common ground subject. For example, one child may remark about a particular book he didn't like—opening the door for the other child to offer an opinion.

Another important concept to explain to your child is "conversation keepers." These are connective phrases that start or keep conversations going in the right direction. Sometimes, they simply parrot what someone has just said, but at other times, they act as bridges to common ground or deeper discussion. Some examples include: "You must have really felt worried when you thought you lost your notebook," "That reminds me of . . . ," "Remember when you were telling the class about . . . ," "Guess what?" or "Can you believe that happened?" Conversation keepers keep conversations going by plugging up talking gaps and showing that the child is tuned in to what is being said. Children can also show they are tuned in by relating the current conversation to something the speaker has said in the past.

Talk with your child about the importance of other communication tools. Eye contact, facial expressions, gestures, body posture and proximity, and movement all communicate the important message that "I am here, and I am paying attention." Eyes that are always averted, even out of shyness, communicate disinterest and a tuning out of the speaker.

Try a Chalk Talk with your child to give him or her some practice in communication skills. You can "set the scene" and pretend that you are a peer so that your child can become more comfortable with conversing. Practice really does help children develop their conversational skills. Also, take advantage of time in the car or at the dinner table to tune up conversations that really go somewhere.

But Not Too Much Conversation

For every shy child struggling to find his or her voice, there is a boisterous child ready to take control of every conversation. Getting a child to stop talking is sometimes even more difficult than getting a child to start talking, but it is every bit as important when staying tuned in to others.

Parents need to be very aware of their child's social skills and talk bluntly yet kindly with their child if they perceive that their child is turning into a "conversation hog"—monopolizing conversation, constantly interrupting, finishing stories other people are telling, or making unrelated comments to turn the conversation in a different direction. The internal coaching message for kids is: "I should not assume that others want to hear me talk a lot." Parents can help their children to not "overtalk" by asking them to have their thinking sides tuned in to the people and conversations around them. The child should understand that it's okay to have pauses in conversation—all empty space does not need to be filled up—and to ask questions that allow others to participate in the conversation.

Again, practice really helps children break bad habits, like inter-rupting, by keeping them tuned in to the conversation.

Stay Tuned In!

The importance of children attending to the world around them is obvious to all parents. Academic and social skills and responsible self-directed behavior depend on being attuned to surroundings. The **Stay Tuned In!** card stresses awareness of social surroundings, especially interactions with peers, because, no matter how good a job you are doing as a parent, peer acceptance has a major impact on your child's developing self-esteem. Children with social skills deficiencies often are unaware of what they are doing wrong since they have not yet developed the observational abilities to compare their skills to others—that's where parents need to step in.

Parents may feel awkward about bringing examples of social lapses to their child's attention. You can use the **Stay Tuned In!** card as a springboard to discuss the importance of staying tuned in. Use the suggestions on the card to help your child develop conversational skills. Chalk Talks, role playing, rehearsal, and discussing real and pretend peer interactions are especially helpful in giving your child a feel for what conversations should sound like.

Chapter 16
FIND THE BRAKES!

Like most kids, you probably have lots of energy to do all sorts of things: play sports, go places, enjoy friends, and have fun. When you put that energy into safe activities at the right time, everything goes smoothly. But sometimes your energy comes out at the wrong times—like at school, the dinner table, or family outings. And sometimes your energy even comes out in dangerous ways—like throwing things that shouldn't be thrown, or letting your behavior get out of control. **"Finding the brakes"** means using your thinking side to control your energy.

Read this talk-to-yourself message to learn how to find the brakes:

Having fun, especially with other kids, gives my reacting side a chance to take control. When that happens, fun can quickly turn into trouble, or even danger. At any point, I may need to **find the brakes** and use them to stop my behavior. I keep my brakes handy by telling myself that fun doesn't mean I turn my thinking side off. I still need to think about my responsibilities, the rules, and what is safe. I need my thinking side even when I'm having fun.

Bottling the Power of Childhood

The energy of childhood is a wonderful thing, but some children struggle with controlling their energy when situations warrant restraint. For example, a child running amok in a restaurant is unacceptable because of concern for the safety and comfort of everyone in the restaurant, including the child. And a child bouncing around in a car, unbuckled, poses a serious danger to the child and others in the car.

Trish's daughter, Shelby, is one such child who had difficulty finding her brakes. Trish said that eight-year-old Shelby would get excited and all wound up and then just couldn't stop. She was "just having fun and running around and around," but Trish would have to step in to say, "That's not OK now," and try to bring her daughter back from the edge. Trish could see that her daughter sometimes had trouble controlling her high energy, so she sat with Shelby to read and discuss the **Find the Brakes!** card. Shelby liked the picture on the card and could easily relate to how the boy realizes almost too late that he better find his brakes. Shelby and Trish now have a common language for the times Shelby is running out of control. Just three quick words, "Find your brakes," are all it takes to remind Shelby of what she needs to do, says Trish.

The Power of Impulse

Sometimes it seems as if children are like little nuclear reactors—once you get them started, they're tough to shut down. When they're young, children have a strong tendency to discharge energy at a sometimes alarming rate. They have very little control over their physical selves. Babies climb to the top of stairs with no understanding of how to get back down. Young children put things into light sockets or pull items off a counter only to have them come crashing down on their heads. Curiosity fuels a lot of this impulsivity, and the physical discharge of energy is an important component of that curiosity—always something else to see, to do, or to get into. Temperament plays a large role in impulsivity. Some children seem always to be in a whirlwind of motion and are constantly getting hurt, causing chaos, or wearing down their parents. Other children may be more tentative and cautious about going out into the world and more fearful of being hurt.

As children grow, most gain more control over their impulses and physical energy. But some children have a difficult time pulling themselves back. These kids take more risks and can be more injury prone—rather than just riding their scooters on the sidewalk, they want to jump off the neighbor's dividing wall. The **Find the Brakes!** card helps risk-taking kids from taking their fun too far.

Why Did You Do That?

When a child has done something particularly reckless—like sliding off the roof into a leaf pile—and has gotten hurt, parents will address their child with a bewildered, "Why did you do that?" to which the response is usually, "I don't know." The roots of such actions and energies can often be found in one of four causes: pure impulse, to impress a peer, to demonstrate mastery, or to retaliate. And impulsiveness can be exacerbated when other children are present. Many parents have commented how their normally "thinking" child loses self-restraint when around other children and becomes reckless.

By the time children reach elementary school, much of their control has been internalized as "directions" for life. Children who are still fueled by impulse stand out against the kids with better brakes. Such children are particularly stimulated by other children and need help controlling their impulses and finding their brakes.

Children working to impress their peers with a "Hey everybody, watch this," often don't stop to think that what they are about to do may be dangerous. They want to fit in with their peer group and constantly one-up the stakes. They want others to follow their lead and also test their own internal limits.

Children working to show mastery of a skill, such as skateboarding, will often attempt tricks beyond their abilities. In their minds, if someone else did it and didn't get hurt, it sets a precedent, and they should be able to do it, too. Such behavior is all part of stretching boundaries and borders, but children forget to remind themselves that they may have to put the brakes on before anyone gets hurt. It doesn't occur to them that there is a risk involved. In the midst of an energy discharge, there is very little if any concern about getting hurt.

Retaliation is another area where impulses and energy can combine with anger to create a potent brew. If two children are in the house and one says, "Tag, you're it," the second child escalates the situation by chasing down the first child, with little regard to the safety of either child, and the result is usually someone tripping and hitting his or her head on the table or some other bad outcome. Parents who leave these situations alone abide by the principle that the kids will "play until somebody cries."

Help Your Child Put on the Brakes

Parents can help their children overcome their impulsivity by asking them to STTA! (pronounced "stay")—Stop, Think, and Think Again. You might want to Chalk Talk different scenarios with your child to help him or her predict the outcomes of potentially dangerous situations:

> **Mom:** Let's say you were riding bikes in the neighborhood with your friends. What if one of your friends wanted to go out of the neighborhood to the store down the street? What would you do?

Son: I don't know.

Mom: Are you allowed to go there?

Son: No.

Mom: Would it be hard to tell your friends that?

Son: Yeah, they might laugh at me.

Mom: Do you remember why you aren't allowed to go there?

Son: Because the street is too busy, and I might get hit by a car.

Mom: That's right. What could you say to your friends that wouldn't embarrass you but would still keep you safe?

Son: Maybe something like, I don't think that's a good idea, because we could get into trouble.

Mom: That's really good. Sometimes we forget to think when we are with our friends and just go along with whatever they want to do, but that can get us into trouble. I like how your answer keeps you safe and out of trouble.

Learning to STTA takes time and practice and requires that kids put their thinking sides in control. When parents are with their children, they can be on the lookout for unsafe ideas or situations. If they are out around town, they can point out what other kids are doing and ask their child to assess the situation. Maybe it's a group of kids riding their bikes without their helmets on or some pre-teens hanging out on a corner smoking. The parent can ask the child what he or she would do in that situation.

Parents also can help their children visualize the idea of finding their brakes. Explain how bikes, cars, motorcycles, airplanes, and practically everything else that "goes" all have brakes to help them stop. Just like those things, your child needs to find his or her brakes. It's helpful for kids to hear stories about their parents and how they did or didn't find the brakes and what happened as a result. Parents can share stories from childhood as well as from the more recent past about times when they maybe should have found their brakes but didn't. For example, "Yesterday, when I yelled at you, what happened wasn't your fault, and I should have found my brakes. I'm still learning, too."

Help your children understand, too, that keeping their physical impulses under control helps them socially. They are more likely to receive invitations to play dates, have more success at school, and be more welcome in the homes and yards of others if they are able to demonstrate that they can make good decisions and use their energy for safe fun.

Find the Brakes!

A child's energy level can sometimes seem limitless. Faced with energetic peers, stimulating environments, or just average daily life, some kids become loud, unruly, and annoying to others. Parents often are provoked to tell out-of-control kids to "stop" or "cut it out" in harsh tones. The anger in a parent's voice may persuade a child to stop, but it won't necessarily reduce the occurrence of these episodes. Using the **Find the Brakes!** card, you can prepare your child for situations that have triggered wild behavior in the past. Try suggesting to your child that he or she should periodically remind himself or herself to "keep the brakes available" when playing or spending time with others. The coaching goal of the **Find the Brakes!** card is to help your child learn to restrain their physical impulses and develop self-control, a critical life skill.

Chapter 17
WATCH OUT FOR YOUR HOOKS!

It's easy to lose track of time while you're having fun. Watching TV, playing video games, using the computer, talking to friends, reading magazines, and stuff like that can become very absorbing. They can **hook** your attention so that important things like homework, chores, or other responsibilities get pushed out of your mind.

Even though it can feel good when you're **"hooked,"** problems develop quickly for kids who let themselves **get hooked**. You can end up in trouble with parents, in school, and even with friends when **your time and attention are hooked**.

Read this talk-to-yourself message to learn how to watch out for your hooks:

Getting **hooked** means doing so much fun stuff that I let other important things slide. It's okay to have fun, but I need to ask myself, "Am I getting too hooked? Are people telling me that I'm going overboard?" I need to **watch out for my hooks** and realize that they may be fun when I'm doing them, but after I stop, it won't be fun to see the people I've disappointed and to face the work I've let go.

Entering "The Zone"

Jeremy, like most children, can spend a lot of time watching TV. When he gets home from school, he likes to relax on his grandmother's couch and shut down. But that relaxing time can easily run into hours if Jeremy's grandmother doesn't intervene. Jeremy, nine years old, is easily hooked on TV. Sandra, his grandmother, said TV soothes him, but it also takes his attention away from what he needs to be doing. For Jeremy, getting hooked meant he wasn't getting his homework done, and that was leading to a lot of stress.

Sandra worked with Jeremy using the **Watch Out for Your Hooks!** card to help him become aware of how he was spending his time and how much time was going by without him even realizing it. Jeremy saw himself in the card's illustration, being tempted by the TV while he had his homework in front of him. He had to work on self-discipline to keep from chucking aside his responsibilities and getting hooked again.

Everybody Gets Hooked

Most adults can relate to children when it comes to the **Watch Out for Your Hooks!** card. Many parents have gone to bed with a book at night, only to stay up until four o'clock in the morning just trying to finish one more chapter, or they've gone on the Internet to research some information and wound up burning three hours online without even realizing it. Kids have hooks, too, and these hooks often can have a lot of power in their lives.

In their early years, children rarely have trouble with getting hooked. Their attention span is fairly short, and most parents don't see their children gravitate unnaturally to something they want to spend a lot of time with or doing. It is not until a child is older, say eight or nine, that this characteristic begins to develop. For example, many children collect trading cards, but some children get hooked on buying more and more. Some children begin to focus on one type of play, even when other options are available to them. Hooked kids get lost in what they are doing, whether it's playing video games, reading a book, watching TV, or talking on the telephone with friends. They lose track of time and responsibility and have difficulty pulling away from whatever has hooked them.

Many of these children like sameness and routines. They often enjoy more solitary activities and prefer a narrow stimulus field where they can see the results of their efforts more easily. These kids can get very absorbed by the things on which they are hooked. If they aren't doing the thing they are hooked on, they are thinking about it or would like to be doing it when they can't. Video games are particularly relevant to some of these children because they can immerse themselves in an entire imaginary world. They can play the game, collect related toys, watch related TV shows, talk with their friends about the game, and build a self-contained universe. It's very easy for them to be diverted from other interests and activities, and this often leads to conflicts with parents.

For example, with a video game, children can enter another world at any time. It's a leap of fantasy that allows them to see themselves as an NBA superstar, a world-class skier, or an armed bandit. The invitation to fantasy appeals to many children and is a powerful one to try and resist. Chat rooms on the Internet are another hook for older children. They can chat with friends for hours saying things they wouldn't say in person, and friendships soon seem to revolve around time spent online.

In and of themselves, activities that can hook kids (or even adults) are not unhealthy. Playing video games, watching TV, or surfing the Internet are not inherently bad. It's when children allow these activities to take over a significant portion of their lives that troubles start to appear. Watching for hooks really involves paying attention and monitoring your child. Ask your child questions like, "What's going on?" "Who are you talking to?" or "How long have you been playing the game?" Helping kids manage their hooks will help parents get their kids back on track.

Helping Your Children Get Unhooked

The best way to help children handle their hooks is to talk about them. Talk with your children about what they are doing—talk about the games and try to understand and compare what they are doing to real life so that they can begin to make links to reality. If your child has a video game hook, you can ask, "I wonder how the developer got the idea for this?" or "Where do the designers come from who work on this stuff?" Ask probing questions, not about the game itself but about the process, and see if you can bring your child out and into a conversation.

Be sure to emphasize that the time the child puts into something demonstrates some good qualities, too, like the child's capacity to learn new material and synthesize new information. Enter into your child's world; connect with the preteen who is busily downloading music from the Internet with questions like, "Do you know what kind of guitar that musician plays? It's a pretty interesting story." Take advantage of connecting opportunities before tackling your child's hooks and then start a conversation with your child about those hooks.

Parents should engage their child in a Chalk Talk and work together to see if they can agree on what their child's hooks are and then come up with a plan to control them. A child's input is especially important because children need to develop a sense of mental monitoring so that they are more conscious of their hooks. Once hooks are identified and a plan is put in place to help a child manage them, parents can support their child's thinking side in a number of ways. For example, a sign posted on a video game might read, "Take charge of where your mind spends its time." Parents can also put kitchen timers by computers and TV sets so that children have a reminder of when their hour is up. Parents should explain to their children that it's okay to have fun, but hooks can ultimately cost a lot in terms of time, peace, and performance.

Watch Out for Your Hooks!

Parents are often frustrated by a child's tendency to be drawn off task or to avoid tasks altogether. Sometimes, this behavior is a deliberate attempt to dodge responsibility. At other times, the source of the difficulty is rooted in a child's attention being easily hooked by appealing toys, books, video games, TV, or other activities. When talking with your children about their hooks, you can first look at the illustration on the Coaching Card to explain how attention gets "caught" by the hooks in life, wasting time and causing trouble. Second, you can enlist your child's help in identifying his or her most enticing hooks: video games, surfing the Internet, watching TV, etc. Third, Chalk Talk with your child about how to self-monitor to stay on task. Provide your child with tools like timers and posted warnings to remind him or her to **Watch Out for Your Hooks!** and pay attention to how he or she is spending time.

Chapter 18
REPAIR THE TEAR

Relationships are like an awesome piece of fabric that offers warmth, protection, and good feelings. But just like pieces of fabric, relationships can tear apart because of problems. Too much arguing, not enough cooperating, and saying mean things can leave you and others feeling angry, hurt, and not wanting to be nice. These problems can **tear the fabric** of your relationships with family members, friends, and teachers. If you don't watch out, your reacting side will make things even worse by blaming others for what's going on. Don't let that happen!

Let your thinking side gain control by reading this talk-to-yourself message:

Right now I feel hurt, but that doesn't mean it's all the other person's fault. I had something to do with what happened, even if it was only the way I reacted to what the person did. I can try to **repair the tear** in our relationship by talking softly, saying something nice like, "I'm sorry, I want us to be friends again," and realizing that the other person probably feels hurt, too.

Love Means Saying You're Sorry

When children are very young, they don't understand the concept of damaging a relationship, much less apologizing for what they've done. If a child hits another child, and the parent forces the child to say "I'm sorry," the sorry will have little meaning for either child. Children's sense of conscience doesn't really begin to develop until the age of four or five, when they begin to understand that other people have feelings and that their actions can have an effect on those feelings.

The illustration on the **Repair the Tear** Coaching Card reflects a child's growing awareness of the impact words and actions have on others. The boy is trying to apologize for something he said or did, but the tear has not been repaired. The rip in the fabric is not yet stitched together, and the girl is not yet ready to accept his apology.

Pam, age 14, can relate very well to the girl in the illustration. She used to be really big on holding grudges and didn't forgive others easily. With family and friends, she used to think she was always right, and it was hard to stop her angry emotions. It was easier for her to hold a grudge than to use her thinking side to repair the tear in her relationship by forgiving or by asking for forgiveness.

Pam says what she didn't see at the time was the big picture—that her behavior was costing her a lot of friendships. Now she realizes it doesn't matter who is right and who is wrong; what matters are her relationships with friends and family. Using the **Repair the Tear** card, Pam has learned to set aside her anger and put her energies toward rebuilding valuable relationships that have been damaged. Sometimes, she's learned, it's as easy as saying "I'm sorry."

Letting Go of Hurt Feelings

The **Repair the Tear** card deals with healing relationships from two different angles—forgiving and offering forgiveness. Sometimes, a child has done something to hurt a friend or family member, and it is up to the child to repair the tear in the relationship. Other times, someone else has hurt the child, and the child must allow the other person to repair the tear rather than hold on to anger and hurt feelings.

When they have made a mistake and damaged a relationship, it is much easier for some children to place the blame on others. They rapidly jump into a defensive mode and become unwilling to accept responsibility for their part in the damage that has been done. Or a child gives lip service to an apology, but from the child's voice and body language, the damaged party knows the attempt is not sincere. And sometimes children can accept responsibility and make a sincere apology, only to have their attempts to repair the tear brushed off or ignored.

You can help your child learn to repair the tear by first explaining to him or her that everyone makes mistakes and does things wrong from time to time. However, the child can turn things around a bit by admitting his or her mistake, saying he or she is sorry, and trying to repair the tear instead of trying to place blame elsewhere. Chalk Talk with your child how making a mistake can take the form of letting a word pop out, forgetting to do a favor, or not doing a chore. These are all good examples of situations where the child may need to repair the tear through honesty, empathy, and an understanding of what he or she did wrong.

Parents can interfere with a child's ability to repair the tear by creating an environment that is too punitive. Such an environment can encourage deceit and make the child go into hiding. The "I'll-teach-you-a-lesson" attitude is more likely to send your child looking for escape routes rather than ways to repair the damage that has been done. Children in these situations can also develop immunity to parental disapproval, with their singular goal being to avoid punishment. Harsh punishment tends to be shortsighted and overrides everything else, making teaching responsibility and accountability difficult. Mistakes should be paired with consequences but also with coaching, to teach the child how to avoid the same mistake in the future.

Another trap parents fall into is the notion that because they warned a child, the child won't make a mistake. Repeated warnings don't always reduce mistakes, but they do build the parent's expectation that mistakes shouldn't and won't be made. Coaching and having Chalk Talks with children will do more to prevent mistakes than simple warnings.

Parent as Referee

Fights between siblings are commonplace, but rather than just letting the kids work it out—a common practice—parents should intervene on behalf of both their children. This isn't the time to be a referee and sort out who did what to whom; this is the time to separate the children before the conflict intensifies and to try to deal with the larger issues that led to the fighting. The parent is not an attorney here, probing for the truth, but is rather a voice of reason. You may say something like, "I know you both were yelling and said things that were hurtful, but let's try to figure out what is really going wrong here. I think that your sister is bored and trying to play with you, but you just want to play by yourself. Is that right?" By dealing with the roots of the problem and not the particulars of the fight itself, parents can help their children repair the tear and strengthen their relationship.

Repair the Tear

Social and emotional skills problems may have a heavy toll on important relationships in a child's life. Expressing responsibility for some of the harm and offering an apology are two ways to help alleviate the damage. The **Repair the Tear** card stresses how children should reflect on the role they played during an encounter and offer a verbal gesture to rebuild the bond.

The open-ended nature of the card's illustration offers the opportunity to Chalk Talk with your child about what he or she imagines took place between the boy and girl, what each might be thinking and feeling, and what the boy could be saying. Because adults are also prone to make damaging comments within relationships, this is a skill message that parents can easily put in practice and then model for children. It's easy for a child's reacting side to take control and hold on to bad feelings, but you can help your child's thinking side understand that relationships are more important than fights, and repairing the fabric of a relationship is more important than holding a grudge or proving who's wrong.

The **Repair the Tear** card is considered the morality card of the Parent Coaching Cards. It deals with issues of right and wrong and stresses the values of honesty, responsibility, and empathy. With this card, parents can help their children emerge from a self-centered world, where they look to avoid responsibility and assign blame, and into a more mature acceptance of the part they play in their relationships.

Chapter 19
THE IMPORTANCE OF QUICK RECOVERY

If you lose something like a backpack or a favorite game, you usually try to find it. While the thing is lost, you feel upset and worried. When you find—or **recover**—whatever you lost, you feel much better. Things are back in their proper place. What a relief!

You can also lose control over you feelings. When this happens, your reacting side may drum up temper tantrums and crying spells. You may sulk and avoid others. Guess what? You can **recover** control of your feelings just like anything else you lose. When you **recover control over your feelings**, you realize things really aren't so bad after all.

You can learn how to recover more quickly by reading this talk-to-yourself message:

That was upsetting and I still feel kind of shaky. I wish it hadn't happened and that I hadn't lost control of my feelings. But I can't change that now. What I can do is take some deep breaths, count to ten, and recover quickly so my upset feelings won't spread to create more problems. **Quick recovery** brings good feelings back and puts bad feelings behind me, where they belong.

Dealing With Life's Disappointments

Children have their emotions challenged every day by the circumstances, events, and people surrounding them. How they handle life's ups and downs—how they recover from disappointment—is the crux of **The Importance of Quick Recovery** card.

Pam, age 14, was a self-professed "drama queen" who was very sensitive to the words and actions of others. When something bad happened, she says, she often responded like it was the worst thing in the world. Pam had difficulty getting control of her emotions and would lash out at others in anger or defensiveness. Critical words could send her into a funk. Pam started to use **The Importance of Quick Recovery** card to help her understand that she could regain control of her emotions and realize that the world wasn't against her. She worked hard to appreciate that her parents were on her side, and that the suggestions they made to her weren't to hurt but to help.

The former drama queen has learned, she says, not to be so defensive and that the world is not going to come to an end if something doesn't go her way. She is learning that even though her emotions can get away from her, she can recover what she's lost and feel better.

The Ability to Recover

Recovery is the process of moving from a state of high emotion to one of relative calm. Recovery is the doorway between an episode of emotional overload and the reestablishment of equilibrium, especially after an outburst of disappointment and frustration. A child's ability to handle disappointment is sometimes evident at an early age. Some infants wail inconsolably, while others are more amenable to settling down and returning to a smoother rhythm. But early temperament is not always predictive of a child's ability to handle emotional letdowns. Some parents see continuity in their child—the easily consoled baby continues that pattern into childhood—but other parents see an "easy" baby turn into a highly emotional child.

An ability to have a quick recovery helps children bounce back from surprises, frustrations, losses, and disappointments. Some children are better able to let go of desires and switch to another interesting activity or possibility. For them, a quick recovery is easily obtained. Other children have a hard time letting go of the thing they cannot have and can spend literally hours awash in the emotional fallout of dashed desires.

It is important for parents to understand that, much of the time, children who have difficulty with a quick recovery really do have emotions that go beyond their control. Parents express frustration at their child's inability to regain control without realizing that control is simply not within the child's grasp. These are children who are riding a rickety boat on a sea of emotion and need their parent's help to get to dry ground. Parents can use **The Importance of Quick Recovery** card to help their children use their thinking sides to recover their lost emotions and steer to calmer waters.

Take a Deep Breath and Count to Ten

Through the course of most days, a child's emotions tend to ebb and flow. But on some days, children find their emotions building to the point where a seemingly meaningless event sets off a flood of tears. For example, some children let frustration build at school, where they are forced into strict time constraints, behavior, and performance standards, and are beset with limits. Over the course of a day, frustration can build, and when the child gets home it all comes out. The child may become demanding—if the child wants something, she wants it now. The child starts to lose control and needs a parent to coach her to the other side of the abyss.

But some parents, caught up with their child in the midst of an emotional meltdown, don't know what to do. They may decide to put the child in her room to "suffer" through it. The parent has to remember that leaving kids by themselves when they can't really process what's going on can do more harm than good. These children have lost control over their emotions—they aren't losing it on purpose, it's just that all reasonable thought is gone—and they need their parent to be the dimmer switch, adjusting the intensity of the emotions, if possible.

You can help your child regain control and reduce the amount of time he or she spends in an emotional black hole in a number of ways. With your touch and voice you can softly soothe your child, or you can rub the child's back to calm him or her. You can have your child take deep breaths and then "blow out" frustration.

Parents also need to control their desire to talk about the situation "right now," as talk can sometimes escalate emotions. The internal coaching message for the parent here is, "I need to think about my timing. I can talk with my child later on after he or she has calmed down." When it is time to talk, the parent should approach the child calmly and say, "I'd like for us to talk about what happened today. Maybe we can work together to figure it out." Using "us" and "we" is better than "you" and "I." The child will feel that you are on his or her side and that you will work together to understand what happened. This type of Chalk Talk can help the child process what happened and plan with the parent how to better avoid it in the future.

Parents can also help their children avoid emotional meltdowns by paying attention to clues and picking up on the little things that tell them a child is heading for trouble. Children should learn to be aware of the way in which they lose control of their emotions and come to their parent for a hug or help. You can help your child with Power Talk like, "It's OK to make a mistake," "Nobody's perfect,"

"It's no big deal, you couldn't control what happened," or "You can try again next time." Power Talk helps children use their thinking side" to better control their emotions.

Does Building Character Have to Be So Hard?

The Importance Of Quick Recovery card reinforces the idea that everyone faces tough times in life, but he or she can bounce back. This notion of resilience is an important one for parents to talk about with their children and model for them. Parents can share stories from their own lives about rebounding from a feeling of upset. Sometimes children may feel they are the only ones who are experiencing pain and disappointment, so it helps them process these feelings more easily if they know they aren't alone.

The idea of character building also begins to take hold in this card. Parents can help their kids understand that everyone has "stuff" to deal with. Managing difficulties helps build tolerance and recovery skills, important character traits on the path to fulfillment and success as an adult. **The Importance of Quick Recovery** card is one of the most important Parent Coaching Cards, something of a prerequisite card to developing other social skills. If a child is not available for coaching because he or she simply can't recover emotionally, the parent may as well be talking to a wall.

The Importance of Quick Recovery

In the midst of an emotional outburst, children must first regain control over their emotions before any learning can take place. **The Importance of Quick Recovery** card offers them the means to do so. Parents can stress that, despite advance preparation, outbursts can't always be prevented. All children and adults will still react with great upset at times. It is during these times that we need to access the emotional skill of recovery. Once control is regained, you might ask your child to leaf through the cards to determine which ones might have prevented the outburst.

The Importance of Quick Recovery card guides children toward an emotional recovery so that they can become better able to engage their thinking sides during a coaching discussion. But don't push if your child is not ready to discuss an incident any further once he or she has recovered. Tell the child, "OK, I need to know when to back off," and try to bring up the subject again at a later time. The emotional skill of recovery is a vital asset because it stems the tide of emotional fallout. A parent can assist their child by referring to this skill during outbursts—"Remember to try for a quick recovery"—and making that recovery of control the central focus of their child's efforts.

Chapter 20
SLOW TO SUCCESS

If you're looking forward to doing something you really want to do, you might rush through whatever you don't want to do. Sometimes there are so many things to do that you may feel as if you won't have enough time to do everything. **Rushing** can cause big problems because when you **rush**, you many lose control over your reacting side. Or, **rushing** through something may mess up how well you do chores, homework, and other stuff like that. When that happens, you usually end up having to do it over again, which ends up taking more time. It can get real frustrating to hear parents and teachers say, "Take your time."

Read this talk-to-yourself message to learn how to slow down:

Rushing through things I don't like doing causes problems. **Slowing down** can actually save me time if I try my hardest to do my best the first time around. I can be much more successful at many more things when I use my thinking side to slow myself down. I do this by telling myself, "Remember, slow down to succeed. I don't always have to race. Doing the very best I can is more important."

Fast, Faster, Fastest

Our culture values speed—fast food, fast Internet connections, one-minute managers, overnight shipping, and the like. But many of the goals that we set for ourselves don't come quickly or easily. Working toward a college degree takes time. Getting physically fit takes effort. Adults can usually differentiate between what can be rushed and what needs our time and attention. Many children, however, cannot. They often are in a rush to complete even critical activities so that they can get on to the next thing or just get done before anybody else. Working toward success requires patience and deliberate effort, skills children must learn over time if they are to understand how to take the measured steps necessary to achieve their goals.

Silvia, age eight, was frustrated by having to slow down to take her "steps" to success. After school, she would rush through her homework so she could get outside to play with her friends. Her homework was often sloppy, incomplete, or simply done wrong because she didn't take the time to read directions and review her work. More often than not, her mother, Juanita, would have to take Silvia to task and have her do her homework over again. Silvia would be angry, but Juanita felt that she had given her daughter fair warning, having told her many times, "Do it right the first time, or you'll have to do it again."

After one too many homework blowups, Juanita began to use the **Slow to Success** card to help Silvia understand that reaching her goal meant taking the success steps to get where she wanted to go. If she tried to jump steps, she might "fall down" or have to start over again. Silvia used her thinking side to realize that rushing only meant more work. Taking her time and working deliberately might seem to take longer, but doing so actually resulted in better quality work and more time with her friends.

The Tortoise vs. the Hare

Thanks to a very slow tortoise and a very quick hare, most children are familiar with the phrase "Slow and steady wins the race." But it's a hard message to internalize for kids because they also know that the only reason the rabbit lost is because he stopped to take a nap. Impressing on children the notion of taking their time to accomplish their tasks can fall on deaf ears for a number of reasons. For younger children, frustration is a common problem. Whether learning to ride a bike or tie their shoes, skills require time and patience to learn—something that most young children have only a limited supply of.

Frustration causes young children to rush through their efforts to minimize the amount of mental and emotional pain caused by the task at hand. Once they show mastery of the skill, however, they will likely spend much more time enjoying the goal they have attained.

When children reach school age, the reasons for rushing through schoolwork and homework take on a new facet. Some children are competitive and want to be the first in their class to finish, regardless of the quality of their work. Other children are not comfortable with the material on which they are working and rush through to get it over with, not thinking that much of the assignment may be done incorrectly. Their fear of failure motivates them to get through their work quickly and not have to deal with what they don't know. Still others want to rush to get to the next project, or recess, or lunch—they just want to move on to the next fun thing.

Slowing Down, Working Toward Success

Getting children to slow down and appreciate what they need to do to accomplish a task well requires that parents begin to teach their children organizational skills, patience, persistence, and the notion that the steps to success are not always easy. Success is not guaranteed, but at least they have a chance if they're willing to tackle the steps.

The first step to success is for parents to model it in their own lives and not to take shortcuts when quality counts. For example, if a child's room needs to be painted, the parent can Chalk Talk about the steps required to get the job done right. Parents can review the **Slow to Success** card with their child and talk about how the boy is climbing the stairs to his goal and how, for the parents, the goal is getting the room painted well.

First, the room has to be cleaned, wallpaper stripped, and rough places sanded down and primed. Taking a step-by-step approach helps a child appreciate that painting a room is a process, and each step has to be taken in turn. If the parent doesn't take the time to cover the carpet and furniture, hours and hours will be spent cleaning up.

As parents work on a task, they can talk with their children about where they are at on the success stairs, saying, for example, "We've got all the prep work done and now we're ready to paint." Parents can also explain to their child that some steps take longer to climb than others—covering furniture is pretty quick, but doing a good job on the trim takes time. By showing children how things are broken down into more manageable steps, children can learn how to incorporate that strategy into their own work.

At first, the parent may need to help their child with breaking down and scheduling activities. For example, a child has to write a report on the Civil War, and the report is due in two weeks. The parent can help the child put his thinking side in charge to break down the assignment into manageable tasks (select topic, do library research, do Web research, make cards with important facts, write outline, etc.) and then schedule a task for each day.

Once the child has practice in breaking down projects, his understanding of the success stairs will begin to improve.

Procrastination Leads to Frustration and Failure

Procrastination is one of the main obstacles kids have to overcome when dealing with more complicated tasks. Children (and adults) often procrastinate when a task seems too large or if it's something they really don't want to do. When kids procrastinate and rush through projects, their reacting side takes over and frustration moves in, setting them up for failure and disappointment. Helping your child see that procrastination is a trap to avoid can help him or her get a good start on the stairs to success.

Failure can also result if a child's goal is unrealistic. Parents can help their child set realistic goals by making it clear what is required to reach the goal and whether or not the child is able to muster the resources to accomplish what needs to be done. Like adults, children will begin to understand that stairs will always be in front of them. Climbing the success stairs helps children appreciate where they came from and gives them a new perspective for what lies ahead.

Dealing With More Challenging Goals

As children get older, demands become greater, tasks become more challenging, and they have to slow down to succeed. When they are young, children may be able to rush through homework and projects that are not too difficult, but as they mature, they have to approach such things more carefully. Children may also give in to their "reacting side" and become frustrated by not being able to reach certain goals until later in life.

An easy trap for parents to fall into is to try to push the child toward her goal by taking steps for her. Parents need to hold themselves back and assess when their child really needs their help and when the child would be better off taking a step on her own. It's important for children to realize that they may not have the resources they need to accomplish their goal, or they may need to get input or ask for help. Parents can help children assess what resources they need to succeed, pitch in when needed, and back away when children have the ability to climb the success stairs on their own.

Slow to Success

Rushing through tasks and activities is typical of most children who tend toward impulsivity. This work style often interferes with their performance, because the children are overly concerned with completing the task rather than with the quality of the job. Parents may unwittingly reinforce this fast-paced approach by telling their children to hurry up or by modeling a beat-the-clock mentality in their own lives. Remember, Parent Coaching Cards work in part by demonstrating how you apply these tools to your own life.

Parents should use the terms on this card immediately before their child begins a task that the child may have rushed through before—usually with a bad result. Refer to the illustration on the card and say, "Remember, slow to success. Goals require us to take one step at a time." These coaching words help your child strengthen the emotional skill of perseverance. As children begin to experience the pride that comes with success, they will be more self-motivated to complete projects with an eye to quality rather than speed. That pride also will act to build in your child willpower, resilience, confidence, and determination—all necessary traits to climbing the stairs of success.

Chapter 21
THINK AND PLAN AHEAD

All kids hit rough spots. Some hit them more often than others. Rough spots are those times when you're caught off guard by something you didn't **plan**. It could be a test you figured was going to be easy but wasn't, or a promise you made but then forgot about. These situations don't happen because of bad luck. They happen when you don't **plan for what's coming tomorrow, or the next day, or the day after that.** Living for the moment may seem exciting and fun, but rough spots eventually come. If you tend to live in the moment, then you've probably found out that bad things happen to kids who don't **think ahead and prepare.**

Read this talk-to-yourself message to help smooth out your rough spots:

Life goes more smoothly when I **think and plan ahead.** My parents and teachers won't bug me so much and I'll feel better about myself. By remembering to ask myself three questions throughout the day, I can make my life run much more smoothly:

1. **What do I have to remember to do today?**

2. **Before I leave this place, do I have everything I need?**

3. **What's coming up in the next few days that I need to prepare for now?**

I Forgot!

Like most preteens, Ryan forgot things—little things, big things, and really important things. Ryan, age 12, had an especially hard time getting from school to home with all of the things he needed to complete homework that was due the next day, as well as papers that needed to be signed by his parents and returned. Ryan wasn't forgetting intentionally, it was just that his lack of organizational skills and tools put him at a disadvantage. He couldn't spontaneously remember everything he needed, but he didn't know how to organize the information so that it was accessible, usable, and timely. Like most kids, Ryan overestimated how much he was able to remember at a moment's notice.

Using the **Think and Plan Ahead** card, Ryan and his mother Anna worked together to come up with a plan to get him organized. She suggested that he jot down notes to himself in his homework planner so that he would know what he needed to bring home to complete projects. Anna would jot down reminder notes for Ryan, too. Ryan also asked for a binder to hold his folders, homework planner, and school supplies. Ryan now plans and gets work done a day or two in advance, something that rarely happened when he was flying by the seat of his pants.

The ability to think and plan ahead is something that most children begin to develop around the age of eight. Prior to this, children have little notion of being on time, being organized, or how long it will take them to accomplish something. Many children have been known to show up at a slumber party with a bag full of toys but no pajamas, toothpaste, toothbrush, or change of clothes. In elementary school, children begin to have a sense of time and planning; for example, they can usually remember to put their lunch in their backpacks for later in the day, though higher-level organizational skills are still developing. As children reach middle school age, they learn to be better managers of their time rather than victims, and they are able to plan for daily and weekly activities with more proficiency.

But not all children learn these organizational skills. Without guidance, they will grow into adulthood as people who are chronically late, who constantly underestimate how long a task will take to complete, and who are irritatingly forgetful. Children—and adults—who display a lack of organizational and time management skills do so at a social and personal cost. They develop a reputation for being someone who can't be trusted or relied on. As adults, they risk becoming people upon whom others cannot depend. Through a lack of planning, they often short-circuit their own lives and find themselves on the receiving end of the frustration and anger of others.

Tools for Planning and Thinking Ahead

Parents often become frustrated by their child's forgetfulness and lack of planning. Children forget the equipment they need for a sports game, the jacket they brought to a restaurant, or the papers they need for school. Parents also seem to be the ones to pay for the mistakes, since they wind up driving home to get the needed supplies, backtracking to the restaurant to retrieve the forgotten jacket, or contacting a teacher to arrange a pickup of misplaced papers. Instead of always rescuing children from their mistakes, parents need to help children learn to become better organized by thinking and planning ahead.

First, the parent should Chalk Talk with their child about the frustrations of forgetting and not planning and the chaos that results. Rather than criticizing the child, the best approach is to say, "How can we work together so you can be more successful?" Remember, some children simply have not developed the skills or do not understand the tools they need to be organized and on time. Children can also benefit from parents pointing out other people who are organized and how it helps them. For example, the parent might say, "Your friend Nate has a pretty neat system to remember what he needs to bring to school each day. He keeps lists and thinks and plans ahead."

Once the problem is brought to light, parents can brainstorm with children on ways their thinking side can help them get organized. Many of the same tools that help adults with their schedules also work for children. Adults can model this behavior by showing children how they keep a calendar for appointments and other activities and how they plan out their day. Parents can also share with their children how planners help them remember what they need, when projects are due, and how to budget their time.

You also can talk with your child about "training" his or her brain to take advantage of downtime to think and plan ahead. Thinking ahead can be done virtually anytime and anywhere. For example, when going up the stairs or walking the dog, children can review what is coming up in their lives. Parents can help their children understand what it means to go through a mental checklist. Practice with your child how that would sound. For example, a parent could say, "When I walk the dog in the morning, I like to think about what I have to do that day. I might remind myself that after work, I need to pick up the dry cleaning and then get your brother from practice. It helps me plan when I think about what I need to do, and that way, I make sure to leave enough time and not run late."

It's important to note that some children aren't very good planners and organizers simply because they haven't had the opportunity to develop these skills. They have become so accustomed to mom or dad telling them where to go, when to be there, and what to bring that they don't trust their own abilities. Parents should prompt their children, but let them carry the responsibility for the work that needs to be done.

The Three Questions

Have a Chalk Talk with your child about getting into the habit of asking himself or herself these three questions every day:

1. What do I have to remember to do today?

2. Before I leave this place, do I have everything I need?

3. What's coming up in the next few days that I need to prepare for now?

Before they head out the door in the morning, have your children review their day to make sure they have everything they need. Keep in mind that certain enjoyable activities, like watching TV or playing video games, compete for the mental space your child needs to get organized in the morning. Be sure children have an ample break between enjoyable activities and heading out the door, so they can get their minds on what needs to be done to get ready to go.

Think and Plan Ahead

If the words "I can't believe you forgot" are a familiar refrain in your household, thinking and planning ahead probably aren't happening too much. Some children need extra help in developing an internal map to guide their decisions and efforts. It seems that no matter how often they must tend to daily responsibilities, they act as if the routine is unfamiliar. To complicate matters further, this directionless demeanor can trigger anger and frustration in a parent and make the child more anxious.

Many parents react to their child's lack of organizational skills by grabbing the "steering wheel" in their child's life. By doing this, they implicitly send the message that the child can't manage his own life responsibly. Instead, the parent should take some deep breaths, start a Chalk Talk by using the messages on the **Think and Plan Ahead** card, and have their child identify the problems without prompting.

Help your child put a plan and the necessary tools in place in order to better think and plan ahead. A parent can certainly offer to help, perhaps by agreeing on checkpoints during the day when the two of you can review the three questions on the **Think and Plan Ahead** card. You may invite your child to request help when needed, but be sure to reinforce any effort toward self-direction. Also, remember that even with the best planning and organizing, things will be forgotten. Have your child work out a plan to correct the mistake and get your help if necessary. For example, if your child has left reference materials at school that will be needed over the weekend, have the child think of some ways to get those materials back—"I could call my teacher at home, or I could go back right now and see if someone is still in the school. Do you think you could drive me?"

Coaching your child in good organizational skills, as well as in the value of thinking and planning ahead, is time well spent. The end result will be a child who feels more in control of his or her life and a parent who feels less frustrated. When your child has moved forward with this skill, you may want to have a discussion about the ingredients for future success in life, and how many of the necessary components come from thinking and planning ahead. Learning to organize and follow through will help your child move ahead on life's path.

Chapter 22
COACHING CHILDREN WITH SPECIAL NEEDS

Many children face special challenges in life, and Parent Coaches need to adjust their coaching styles and strategies to fit the individual needs of their children. This is, of course, not a comprehensive reference, but it should give parents some additional assistance in coaching their child, regardless of the circumstances surrounding their child's abilities. Here we will address the special needs of children with ADD or ADHD (attention deficit disorder or attention deficit hyperactivity disorder), children with Asperger Syndrome (AS), children who are anxious, children who are defiant, and children with physical disabilities.

Children With ADD or ADHD

The Parent Coaching Cards were originally developed for families who have children with ADD or ADHD to help them coach their kids in social and emotional skills. The cards provide the repetition of lessons that is so important to children affected by ADD or ADHD. These children have steeper and longer learning curves, make mistakes more frequently, and require more repetition for learning. These children are flooded with emotions and external "light and noise." The pull of the environment surrounding them is quite great, and they often have a difficult time using good judgment when around their peers. They have more hurdles to overcome, including the emotions of their own parents. Parents of these kids are especially prone to act out of frustration toward their children because their own patience has been worn down.

Taking a step back and taking time to reevaluate parenting skills may be difficult, but important to do if parents are to successfully coach their children. A challenge for families dealing with ADD or ADHD is that the parent has become so reactive and quick to punish that the child spends a lot of time covering his or her tracks to stay out of trouble; the parent sometimes just doesn't know where to begin coaching. The self-esteem of these children is often fragile, so parents have to tread carefully. The coaching approach is just as important as the coaching message.

Parents of children with ADD or ADHD are wise to consider an approach where the consequences of behavior are paired with coaching. Sometimes it helps to have a Parent Coaching mantra in the midst of chaos, such as "Coach first, consequences later," to remind parents of what they need to do.

For the child, a personal Coaching Journal is a wonderful place to start. Journaling can help the child understand cause and effect as well as coaching and consequences. For example, if a child got into a fight with another child because of name-calling, the parent can sit down and review the **Don't Take the Bait!** card. Then, have the child write an entry in his or her journal using the idea of STOP—Situation, Trap, Outcome, Plan to Prevent. The child can write what the situation was (I was at lunch with my friends); how the trap was set (Mike was saying mean things about some people); what the outcome was (I said something mean and got into trouble); and how the child plans to prevent it in the future (when I'm around my friend Mike, I'll work hard not to take the bait).

You can also have your child write "pledges" dealing with different situations. For example, a card with a "Smart Play Pledge" can remind the child how he or she is expected to play at a friend's house:

SMART PLAY PLEDGE

I, Michael, realize that when I get together with other kids, I sometimes turn my thinking side off. Bad ideas come into my mind, and when I follow those ideas, I get into trouble. Fun doesn't have to be dangerous or get me into trouble. When I play, I will keep my thinking side turned on and watch out for bad ideas that could ruin my fun.

Parent and child can put together pledges for school, sports, lessons, or other social situations. Before the child leaves for the engagement, have the child read the card and sign it. The repetition helps remind children of their responsibilities.

Parent Coaching Cards that are particularly valuable for children with ADD or ADHD include **Find the Brakes!; Don't Take the Bait!; Stay Tuned In!; When Words Pop Out, Watch Out!;** and **Know When to Back Off!**

Children With Asperger Syndrome

Children with Asperger Syndrome (AS) have special difficulty tuning in to the social undercurrents of the world around them. They don't fully understand or experience emotions like empathy, their conversational skills are lacking, and the world seems like a big puzzle to them with lots of missing pieces. When talking with others, their comments don't fit in with the flow of conversation. When others express an opinion, they will counter with facts and have difficulty with developing opinions of their own. Kids with AS are very rooted in facts—talk about dinosaurs, and these "little professors" can bombard you with details. Express opinions or try to have them express an opinion, and they have a difficult time pulling one together.

Parents of children with AS can help them develop appropriate conversational skills by working with them on the ideas presented in the **Stay Tuned In!** card. Together they can practice conversation openers, finding common ground, and how they can pay attention to the environment around them to stay rooted. Children with AS learn more easily through illustrations, and parents can use the illustrations on the cards to talk about social rules. For example, parents can ask what the kids on the **Know When to Back Off!** card might say to each other, and then ask what their children would say in the same situation. Practicing the words in a very practical manner helps children with AS understand what is expected in everyday conversation. Chalk Talks can also play an important part in developing these social skills.

Kids with AS also tend to be very concrete. Symbolism, like that in **Don't Take the Bait!** can be confusing, so parents will want to take the time to explain how certain things like video games or TV can control children if children don't control them.

Children with AS are challenged by the world mainly because they don't understand the little nuances in everyday life. For example, if a friend is upset, the child with AS may think that getting her friend to laugh with a joke may be the best way to make him feel better. Assessing social situations—taking into consideration a person's tone of voice, stance, words, and facial expressions—is simply not something these children do naturally.

One way parents can help their kids tune in to what's around them is to practice with pen and paper. Parents can draw a stick figure of a child with an angry or sad expression, put an empty word bubble above the figure, and have the child fill in the dialogue. Ask your child, "What would you say? What would you say next?" Taking little steps can help children with AS move forward in better understanding their social skills and developing a higher level of social awareness.

Children Who Are Anxious

Children who are anxious are children who worry over "what might happens" and have not learned how to effectively sooth themselves. These children are awash in a sea of anxiety without an anchor, at the mercy of the constantly shifting tides of life. They tend to believe they have no control and frequently imagine the worst outcome for various situations.

For example, a child drops a lunch tray in school. Alison, who is anxious, sees this and becomes fearful of buying hot lunch. She worries excessively that she may drop her tray and imagines the horrible outcomes—embarrassment, humiliation, and other kids laughing at her. One experience, even if it's not their own, can leave a lasting trace in the mind of children who are anxious and keep them from taking action in the future.

A wonderful tool for parents to use with these children is an audiotape. With scripted messages, parents can become their child's thinking side, and the child can play a tape over and over again to help sooth them and provide the missing emotional anchor that will keep the child from feeling so adrift. For example, one tape may focus on **Beat the Fear!** skills and talk to the child about how he or she is going to get in line to buy lunch without letting worried thoughts get in the way. The parent can talk to the child about how the thinking side wants him to be a big boy, but the worried side wants to keep him eating peanut butter and jelly sandwiches every day. Tapes can be just one or two minutes long and can specifically address a child's particular fears or simply reinforce the child with positive thoughts for the day.

Parents can even go so far as to have their children practice or be exposed to the things that they are anxious about at home. Dropping a tray of food in the kitchen shows them that the world will not end in catastrophe. It is the fear of an event that is so debilitating to these children, not the event itself. If they can be shown that something isn't as bad as they've made it out to be, their fear will diminish.

Cards that are particularly important for these children include: **Beat the Fear!**, **The Importance of a Quick Recovery**, and **Slow to Success**.

Children Who Are Defiant

Children who are defiant are hard to coach because they typically have a greater than normal need to assert their autonomy. The key to using the Parent Coaching Cards with these children is that they not perceive the cards as instruments of parental control. These are kids who, on the surface, disregard parental approval and don't care about parental disapproval. But deep down, they really do care, and that caring has to be slowly and carefully drawn out.

Parents have to be very gentle with children who are defiant because they are very touchy and prickly—like little porcupines—and combine oversensitivity with a propensity for rushing to judgment. They are particularly good at punishing parents by denying cooperation.

It is also important that an adversarial relationship doesn't develop between parent and child. For example, after the child has come through a bad situation, the parent can take the child aside and revisit the "scene," asking what the child could have done differently, reflecting on other possible outcomes, and helping the child process the situation to see how things really could have ended up the way the child wanted them.

Parents also have to be prepared to take responsibility for their part in a child's behavior. For example, when they overreact to a minor offense, parents must be willing to accept feedback from their child. Learning patience and serenity goes a long way in calming defiance and helping the child get back to a place where parent and child can work together.

Important cards for this group of children include: **Cooperation!**; **The Importance of Quick Recovery; When Words Pop Out, Watch Out!**; and **Don't Take the Bait!**

Children With Physical Disabilities

Children with physical disabilities (auditory, visual, mobility-based, or other) are faced with a complex set of circumstances. Their disability sets them apart from other children and activities, their parents tend to be highly protective, and they face a higher number of day-to-day challenges in the simple acts of living.

These children sometimes can be socially isolated, and, as a result, when they are out in the world, they don't have much experience to draw on in terms of social interactions. Their feelings of anger, frustration, and oversensitivity can also interfere with their ability to develop friendships outside of a safe circle. Parents should use the Parent Coaching Cards to help these children bridge the gap between themselves and their peers by teaching the social skills they may not have had an opportunity to develop.

Two areas in particular can be especially rewarding for children with disabilities to work on—being honest and open about their disability and being able to comfortably ask for and accept assistance.

At home, parents of children with disabilities provide a bubble of protection that shields children from many of the experiences they may have in school or other social settings. The parent intuitively knows what the child needs, and the child rarely has to ask for help. The parent is also keenly aware of their child's disability and the special circumstances that surround that challenge. However, in a school setting, other adults and children may not be aware of the child's disability or the extent to which it affects the child's everyday life. By communicating clearly with the community around them, children with disabilities can help others understand what their special needs are and how to interact with them in a way that is positive, productive, and helpful. For example, if a child has difficulty hearing out of her left ear, she may want to explain to friends: "I can hear you better when you talk in my right ear because my left ear doesn't work so good." This sharing is not to satisfy others' curiosity, but is, rather, to create understanding. It shows that the child has power over the disability.

Parents also can use Chalk Talks to help their children learn how to ask for help when they need it. Many children, and children with disabilities are no exception, are embarrassed to ask for help and would rather suffer in silence than let on that anything is wrong. This important skill is one all children should master—knowing when they have gone past their abilities or resources and need help. Parents can make up their own **Know When to Ask For Help** card as well as other cards that address their children's special needs.

Other cards that are important for children with physical disabilities include: **Stay Tuned In!**; **Cooperation!**; **Don't Trust Your Jealous Feelings!**; **When Words Pop Out, Watch Out!**; and **Step Into Your Cantaloupe Skin!**

Find Your Special Coaching Style

As with other kids, coaching children with special needs requires parents to find a style that meets the requirements of their children. When establishing a coaching approach, the parent needs to first look for an entry point from which a dialogue can be developed. For example, a child may suddenly express the thought that he can't do anything right, and that he feels powerless to do anything about it. The child is letting the parent peer into his insecurities and also asking for help. Parents may want to jump right in with Parent Coaching advice, but they should first express an understanding of the child's feelings. For example, a parent could reply, "I understand you feel that way, and I feel bad for you, but I think the two of us could figure this out if we put our heads together." This reinforces the team alliance and shows the child that the parents are on his side.

Parents also need to find their coaching voice, a key component in effective communication with their child. Many parents say the right things, but the tone and volume of their voice communicate something else. Children are very sensitive to the parent's voice, which needs to come from the heart and the head. When parents speak with love and understanding, even when they are disappointed in a child, the connection between the two will remain unbroken. Parents need to remember that they have thinking sides and reacting sides, too, and how they use them with their children will greatly affect the quality of their relationship and the development of their child.

Chapter 23
COACHING IN THE CLASSROOM

Parent Coaching Cards have wide application in many aspects of a child's life, including school. School presents countless challenging situations for children: Pressure to fit in with friends (even when those friends are engaging in inappropriate behavior), clowning in the classroom, hurt feelings, bullying, and so much more. Actively incorporating the Parent Coaching Cards into school life can play an important part in building children's social and emotional skills.

Parents and teachers can use Parent Coaching Cards in the classroom in three ways—preventively, to address past behavioral problems, and as an alternative to punitive-based solutions. If you plan to work with your child's teacher on using the Parent Coaching Cards in the classroom, you should first meet with the teacher to discuss what the cards are, how the cards are used at home, and to give the teacher the opportunity to review the cards so that you are speaking with a common language. Some teachers may use the cards individually with a student, or they may opt for a more proactive approach and use the cards as a basis for classroom discussions on social and emotional skills.

Michael Doesn't Take the Bait

Dawn, mother of nine-year-old Michael, had begun using the Parent Coaching Cards in hopes of helping Michael develop his social skills. Michael, who has ADHD, was caught up in a relentless cycle of "crime and punishment" at school because of behavioral problems, such as fighting. The first two cards Michael and Dawn worked on were the **Thinking Side and Reacting Side** and **Don't Take the Bait!** One of Michael's biggest challenges, Dawn said, was learning not to take the bait when other children tried to get him to fight. Within two days of reviewing the Parent Coaching Cards, Michael came home with a wonderful success story.

Michael had once again been approached by some boys who wanted him to go fight another child with them. He remembered the **Don't Take the Bait!** card and told the other children, "No, I will not fight; it will just get me into trouble." He then went outside to find another friend to play with on the swings, ignoring repeated requests to join in the fight. Michael's parents wrote a letter to the school's principal expressing concern over the recess situation and relating how Michael had made a good choice. Dawn also shared the Parent Coaching Cards with Michael's school counselor, so the counselor and Michael's teacher could reinforce at school the work being done at home.

Heading Them Off at the Pass

Children are often blindsided by tricky situations at school that they just didn't see coming, even though they may have faced similar situations before. Parents and teachers can prepare students for these situations by using the Parent Coaching Cards as a preemptive strike against bad decisions and poor choices.

For parents, it's important to have conversations with their children about situations in school that are particularly treacherous environmental triggers. For example, if you know your child is having a substitute teacher, and you know your child tends to clown around and get in trouble when there is a substitute teacher, you can review the **Quit the Clowning!** card and discuss how it applies to your child's behavior around a substitute teacher. If your child's feelings are easily hurt, or your child has trouble in P.E. class, a good card to review might be **Step Into Your Cantaloupe Skin!** You can also ask your child to go through the cards with you and pick out ones he or she thinks might apply in different situations. Each day, spend five or ten minutes reviewing the cards and their messages to help your child use his or her thinking side when faced with challenges at school.

For teachers, cards can be used more generically as tools to improve the overall behavioral skills in the classroom. The teacher can pick one or two cards each week to review with the class—starting with the **Thinking Side and Reacting Side** card—and to play some Coaching Card games (see appendix). The teacher should try to incorporate the cards' catch phrases into the classroom lingo.

Connie, a school counselor in Pennsylvania, uses the cards with her classroom groups. She notes that her classes are very motivated to learn the different cards, apply their "traps" to the cards, and share experiences from their own lives. Connie uses role playing in her classes and has each student make a Coaching Journal with STOP strategy sheets that they can use to evaluate tough-times situations and make a plan for next time. One key phrase she has incorporated into her classes is "thinking or reacting side." Kids are able to visualize this and realize that using their thinking sides puts the power in their hands, remarks Connie. When she says, "Which is in control, your thinking or reacting side?" the children really understand. Connie has even used this self-talk on herself—it's powerful!

Using Coaching Cards to Modify Past and Present Behavior

If a parent or teacher is dealing with a child who repeatedly demonstrates a specific behavioral problem, the Parent Coaching Cards can be used to help the child understand the root of the problem and what to do to fix it. Many school-aged children, for example, have a problem with bossiness. If the teacher is giving instructions, the bossy child may "report" to the teacher when so-and-so isn't doing his or her work right. These children often over-step their boundaries and are controlling of other children. In this situation, the teacher and parent should discuss privately the **Know When to Back Off!** card with the child.

The parents and teacher work together to reinforce the message, reminding the child to think about what happens when he or she reports the behavior of others. To help the child remember the message, the teacher may tape the catchphrase or even the card to the child's desk. This visual reminder keeps the child's thinking side in charge when the reacting side is itching to let loose.

Teachers and parents can also incorporate the Parent Coaching Cards into a child's Individualized Education Plan (IEP), where goals can be specified and outcomes measured. For example, the Coaching Huddle form on the following page can be used as a type of "Behavior Lesson Planner" for corrective discipline. Students use the form to reflect on their behavior and to document it, and they use the Coaching Cards to identify ways the behavior can be corrected. The teacher can then review the form and revise if indicated. Integrating the forms into the student's Coaching Journal can supplement other strategies in his or her IEP.

COACHING HUDDLE FORM

1. My Trigger:

2. Skills Needed to Control My Trigger:

3. Tool(s) to Improve Skills:

4. What My Coach Will Do to Help Me Coach Myself:

Corrective Actions Usually Fare Better Than Punitive Ones

For Michael, near constant punishment for misbehaving at school wasn't helping to change the basic problem: He did not have the social skills to handle his environmental triggers, and punishment for his actions seemed only to escalate his problems and damage his self-esteem. Using the Parent Coaching Cards, his parents started to change Michael's reactions to his environment. His parents were using the cards both as preventive tools and as tools to modify existing behavior. Teachers and parents can also use the cards as an alternative to punitive responses to problem behaviors.

Punitive-based problem solving often results in an antagonistic relationship between the child and the teacher. Focusing instead on what can be done differently to prevent the problem in the future helps the child build a skill set and helps the teacher improve overall behavior in the classroom. An example of this is the child who calls another child a name. Rather than a time-out in the hallway or a trip to the principal's office, the teacher can have the child review the **When Words Pop Out, Watch Out!** card and write an entry in his or her Coaching Journal that tells what happened and what could have been done differently to achieve a better outcome. This activity helps the child better understand his or her actions and learn how to make smarter choices when faced with similar situations in the future.

Working as a Team Brings Positive Results

Teachers and parents both want the same thing for children—success in school. Parents want to feel that their children have the support of their teachers and are in a climate where they can excel. Teachers want to have eager learners and students who are respectful and considerate of others. Parent Coaching Cards are a shared tool parents and teachers can use to reinforce the lessons the child is learning in social and emotional skills and management.

The cards can be used preventively, to deal with ongoing behavioral problems, and as an alternative to punitive-based solutions. They are portable and flexible—they can be carried in a backpack or taped to a child's desk as a reminder—and teachers can individualize the cards to address the special concerns of each child. This child-friendly tool speaks to kids directly and helps them understand their thinking and reacting sides, leading them to achieve greater success in the school environment.

PARENT COACHING GAMES

There are many ways to incorporate the Parent Coaching Cards into family life to help children learn and develop the social skills on which the cards are based. Families can read and discuss the cards at the dinner table, in the car, individually, or as situations warrant a review of a particular card's meaning. Children also learn more readily when important information is presented in a game format. Here are six games Parent Coaches can play with their kids to encourage them to use their thinking side to learn about and understand the concepts underlying the Parent Coaching Cards. These games can also be modified for a classroom setting.

Taking Turns Being the Coach

Family or group members are paired together to tell a real (or pretend) tough-time story to each other, with the other member supplying coaching. The coaching comes in the form of providing a helpful talk-to-yourself message or a Parent Coaching Card message. Next, the pair alternates roles. This activity plants the foundation for children to accept coaching from others, such as parents and teachers, and also to offer feedback to the coach about whether the coaching was easy or hard to understand.

Coaching Card Concentration

Read excerpts from individual Coaching Cards and ask your child to identify which cards they are from. For example, read, "It's okay to have fun, but I need to ask myself, 'Am I getting too hooked? Are people telling me that I'm going overboard?'" Ask your child to identify the correct card. Do the same for each card.

Coaching Card Game Show

The parent or another adult is the game show host and the children are the contestants. The parent reads a pretend tough-time story and makes believe that it's written in a letter sent by a kid from another city. The contestants must listen carefully to the story and then try to figure out the best Coaching Card to solve the person's problem. They have 30 seconds to write the Coaching Card name on a sheet of paper.

For example, Bobby from Birmingham writes:

"Every time I get on the bus the kids call me 'buck-teeth beaver' because my two front teeth really stick out. It really gets me. What should I do?"

Or, Sarah from Seattle writes:

"My girlfriend is always getting new stuff, and my parents don't buy me much. When I go over to her house I feel like I'm walking into a toy store! I can't stand it! What should I do?"

Parents can come up with other scenarios and see which cards their kids think are appropriate. Parents can give points to their children depending on their responses.

Clues and Instructions

Talk with children about clues and instructions, emphasizing how they need to take their clues from their environment and use those clues to give themselves instructions about appropriate behavior.

Give children clues and ask them what their self-instruction should be. Here are some sample clues and instructions to get started.

Clue: Kids talking quietly at recess, backs turned away from the crowd.

Self-Instruction: I should respect their privacy.

Clue: You are behind a younger kid at the top of the slide but the kid refuses to go down.

Self-Instruction: Maybe the kid is scared, so I'll try to help, but I definitely won't push the kid down. If I have to, I'll just climb back down the ladder.

Clue: While playing basketball, a girl on the sideline picks up the ball and won't give it back.

Self-Instruction: Maybe she just wants to play. If I'm nice to her, maybe she'll give it back. If that doesn't work, I can always get help.

What's the Judgment Call?

Judgment is another word for the instructions that kids give themselves and the decisions they make when they are in different situations. Your child can play this game alone, or you can divide a group of children into teams. The parent tells the child the situation, and the child has two minutes to figure out the best decision, or judgment call, for the person in the story to make. At the end of two minutes, ask each child or team to give a one-sentence answer to the judgment call.

For example, try the following situation:

> Your friend, whom you really like, surprises you by calling you a bad name in front of another kid whom you don't know that well. You realize that your friend is not joking around. What's the judgment call? Some better judgment calls include walking away, telling your friend that you will talk about it later with him or her, and asking your friend if there is something bothering him or her.

The parent can make up situations and award three points for the best judgment call and one or two points for other satisfactory answers. Some other scenarios you can use include:

- You are in the cafeteria when your best friend sticks two potato chips in his ears. Everybody starts cracking up, and he hands you a potato chip to put in your ear.

- You didn't do your homework assignment, and you lie to your teacher when she asks you for it. You tell her you forgot it at home when, in truth, you didn't get it done because you were watching TV.

- A family is coming over for dinner, and you really don't like the kid who is your age. You wish it wasn't going to happen and are angry with your parents for inviting them over.

- You're in line at school when another kid butts right in front of you to stand next to a friend.

- You overhear your teacher tell another teacher something private about a student who you really don't like.

- While walking outside to the playground, you trip into another kid by accident. The other kid pushes you hard and you fall on the ground.

- You are taking a test and realize that one of your best friends is copying some of your answers.

- You want to make friends with a new girl in school since she seems nice, but you don't know very much about her.

Make Your Own Coaching Cards

The Parent Coaching Card set includes 20 different cards that cover a broad range of social and emotional skills, but you may find a situation in your family that is not addressed on any of the cards. Work with your child to develop and design Coaching Cards that meet the special needs of your family. Chalk Talk with your child about the situation, come up with thinking and reacting responses, and then have your child work out a talk-to-yourself message that would be meaningful to him or her. Your child can also draw a picture on the front of the card to reflect the situation as he or she sees it and to convey the emotions that are involved. See the next two pages for examples of child-created cards.

Sample child-created Coaching Card:

Don't Play Tricks on Others or It Will Backfire on You

Sometimes we have a chance to play tricks on others such as playing ding-dong-ditch. It can happen when our parents leave us alone and we get the itch to play a trick.

Before you do that, read this talk-to-yourself message:

I need to think first about what trouble I might get into for the trick I want to do on others. Is it worth getting caught and being grounded? Probably not!!

©Jesse A. & Dr. Steve, 1998

Sample child-created Coaching Card:

Timing

You use this skill when needing attention or affection with friends or parents. For example you come home from school and your mom is on the phone. You just got an A on your math test. Your dying to tell her the good news. One thing not to do is say, "Mom, mom I got an A on my math test! Get off the phone!" What you do instead is say to yourself:

"I better wait till she gets off the phone, that way my grade will be better appreciated and I'll get a better response."

There are many ways that this applies with friends—if they are busy or not in a good mood, don't interrupt them. Later on they will appreciate you because you let them have time to themselves.

©Pamela 1999

Typed and composed by myself with a little help!

PARENT COACHING CARDS

Parent Coaching Cards are available as a set of 20 4" x 6" full-color, coated cards, gathered on a key ring for easy use. See and order them at www.parentcoachcards.com. The set includes a short instruction booklet for parents and a full-size coloring book to enhance the effectiveness of the cards with younger children.

The cards usually cost $29.95, but purchasers of this book may use the coupon on this page for $5.00 off the price.

Send a check or money order to: **Parent Coaching Cards, P.O. Box 1263, Blue Bell, PA 19462.** Please add $4.00 for shipping and handling, plus $1.80 state tax per set if you are a Pennsylvania resident.

If you order on the Web site (www.parentcoachcards.com), enter code "PCC" to receive the $5.00 discount.

You may also request additional information and receive Dr. Richfield's monthly e-mail parenting column by sending your name and e-mail address to director@parentcoachcards.com. Dr. Richfield is available to speak to groups about Parent Coaching Cards and how to coach social and emotional skills to children of all ages. Please e-mail him for further information.

$5 PARENT COACHING CARDS COUPON

Mail a copy of this coupon with your order for $5.00 off the price of the Parent Coaching Cards.

MORE GREAT RESOURCES FOR PARENTS FROM SOPRIS WEST

Going for the Gold
A Parent's Playbook for Behavior Change
W. Jean Cronin, PhD and Linda M. Bessire, EdD

By incorporating game-like methods into daily routines, you can create positive change in your child's behavior! This book breaks down complicated research and delivers easy to use techniques to parents who need help with a "not so perfect" child. As family life improves, so will your child's odds of developing healthy relationships in the future!

165GOLD (55 pages and 5 forms) Grades 1-6

Why Don't They Like Me?
Helping Your Child Make and Keep Friends
Susan M. Sheridan, PhD

It's heartbreaking to know your child has trouble making friends, but what can you do? This book offers a practical approach that helps parents teach their children the social skills they need to develop friendships—like starting conversations, joining in, and controlling anger. Plenty of examples, how-to steps, and role-plays make these techniques easy to teach and fun for both you and your child.

25LIKEME (188 pages) Grades 1-6

The Tough Kid Parent Book: Why Me?
Practical Solutions to Tough Childhood Problems
William R. Jenson, PhD, Ginger Rhode, PhD, and Melanie Hepworth Neville, MA

This book uses a realistic and proactive approach to handling children's difficult behaviors—like arguing and noncompliance. Parents will learn how to help children establish regular routines of getting up on time, doing household chores, completing homework, etc. while they create better family relationships and an important link between home and school. (A CD-ROM with reproducible forms is included.)

194PAR (192 pages) Ages 3–13

To order, or for more information, contact Sopris West . . .
1-800-547-6747 or visit our Web site www.sopriswest.com

THINKING SIDE AND REACTING SIDE

CAN'T ALWAYS GET WHAT YOU WANT!

Our brains help us think about the things we do every day—like how to do home-work, when to ask for something, and other stuff like that. **This thinking side is what "thinks" us through problems and helps us learn how to succeed at life.**

There's also a part that reacts to the world around us—like when we shriek with excitement on a roller coaster ride or yell with anger if things don't go our way. This **reacting side** lets us have many kinds of feelings, good as well as bad.

Usually, our **thinking side** and **reacting side** work together just fine. But sometimes our **reacting side** grabs control over our **thinking side.** When this happens, anger, stubborn-ness, jealousy, and other funky feelings can cause us to say and do stuff that creates all sorts of hassles. This is why it's much better to let your **thinking side** stay in charge and to keep your **reacting side** under control.

These cards will help you do this by teaching you how to think your way through problems you may face at home, school, and with friends. First, each card will teach you about when to use it. Then, it will suggest a **talk-to-yourself message** that you can read, or have some-one read to you. As you read these messages, try repeating them in your own mind so your **thinking side** can learn them.

There are times in life when you get to visit great places, receive great gifts, and have great times with family and friends. These times fill you up with feelings of love and happiness. Then, there are times when **you don't get what you want.** You may end up feeling so angry and empty that it becomes tough to remember all the times you felt totally filled up. When this happens, your reacting side may cause you to hurt others with angry words and actions. But, this just causes more problems—like getting punished for your mean behavior.

To stop this cycle, read this talk-to-yourself message:

Sometimes I get what I want and sometimes I don't. Just like my favorite TV shows, even good things have built-in endings. My thinking side can prepare me for endings and the times I won't get what I want. I can decide to remember a favorite time when I felt really filled up. This happy memory of being filled with good feelings can help push away the angry and empty ones.

Clowning around seems fun and gets laughs. You may act silly to get attention or impress others, but it doesn't always work out that way. **Clowning around can backfire.** Sometimes it backfires at school, getting you in trouble with teachers. Sometimes it backfires with other kids, who think you're too weird to be around. This makes you feel bad about yourself and there's nothing funny about that!

The quicker you learn to **quit the clowning,** the quicker others will see you as mature and not so hungry for attention.

Turn off your silly side and turn on your thinking side by reading this talk-to-yourself message:

Silly behavior just doesn't blend with most people and places. Life goes much better when I act my age. My **clowning around** might make me and maybe a few other kids crack up laughing, but it wrecks my chances with most people. My thinking side can help me keep a lid on the silliness and help me know when it's perfectly okay to clown around. I can learn more mature ways of getting noticed by watching how non-silly kids do it.

How many times has this happened to you? You're bugged by something going on. Maybe you feel angry and before you know it, words **pop out** that land you in deep trouble. Or, something seems kind of funny and before you know it, you say something as a joke. Another person, usually an adult, like a parent, teacher, or coach, doesn't agree about the funny part. It doesn't even help to say, "I was just kidding around."

These situations happen when wrong words **pop out** before your thinking side can decide if it's really a good idea to say them.

Read this talk-to-yourself message to learn how to stop wrong words from causing trouble:

It's okay to share ideas and feelings, as long as I choose the right time and right words. When I let my reacting side speak for me, wrong words usually **pop out.** These wrong words lead me to time-out or some other punishment. My thinking side can help me find the right words, or remind me that sometimes I just need to keep quiet. I can be on the lookout and stop wrong words before they **pop out.**

There are loads of things in life that can upset you—being teased, having trouble with homework, not being invited to a party, and other stuff like that. When you have your "banana skin" on, you **easily feel bruised.** You probably spend time feeling bad and acting angry. Sometimes your reacting side makes you want to hurt others back so you're not the only one feeling crummy. But this only makes things worse.

If you see something that bruises heading your way, try dealing with it by reading this talk-to-yourself message:

I can't expect success all the time. Hard times are a part of everyone's life. I must remember that although I feel bad when things don't work out, I am not a bad person. I do plenty of things just fine and people notice my strengths. I need to remember my successes right now, the pride I can feel, and all the good things others believe about me. **I can use this pride and grow a thicker "cantaloupe skin"** to prepare for what's coming. My thinking side will help me do this.

Life is filled with all sorts of situations that may lead to trouble. Things may happen at a friend's house, when you're playing outside with a group, while watching TV with a brother or sister, or even at school. Maybe someone calls you a name or dares you to follow him into bad behavior. Maybe you see some dangerous fun that's hard to resist.

If you let them, **these situations will bait you**—just like a hooked worm baits a fish. Before you even know it, you've been baited into wrong action or a bad decision.

You may not even know you've taken the bait until it's too late, so it's a good idea to review this talk-to-yourself message from time to time:

I have to be on the lookout so I don't get **baited into** behaving badly. Getting **baited** can happen anytime, anywhere—and with anybody. One way to prevent this from happening is to stop and ask myself, "Am I being **baited** right now?"

If the answer is "yes," or even "maybe," stop. Do not follow the other person's lead. Don't let yourself react to whatever is happening at that moment. Give yourself time to think it through some more, or to talk the situation over with someone you trust. **Don't take the bait!**

SHOW YOUR L♥VE FOR PEOPLE, NOT JUST FOR STUFF!

DON'T TRUST YOUR JEALOUS FEELINGS!

Life is filled with all kinds of stuff to do and see—great toys, awesome video games, cool TV shows, and fun activities. These things can make you feel good and totally filled up while doing them. That's OK! Having fun is one of the terrific things about life. **But it's not the only thing.**

Sometimes your interest in stuff can cause you to close off from people. That's not good for you and doesn't make them feel so great, either.

If your mind gets trapped in a tunnel of stuff, read this talk-to-yourself message as a reminder to keep showing your love for others:

Even though great stuff makes me feel filled up, all fun stops at some point. But **my love for others and their love for me doesn't ever end.** It's always there, deep inside, even though I might not be thinking about it. My thinking side can help me out of a tunnel of stuff. My thinking side reminds me to find ways to **show my love**—taking time to talk with my family, give hugs, write a note, or do something helpful without being asked.

Being around other kids, especially friends, brothers, and sisters, can trigger strong feelings of jealousy. Maybe you see what they have, or the way your parents treat them. Sometimes it seems like other kids have better things, or are getting treated like they're superspecial. **Jealous** feelings can make you focus only on what you don't have. When **jealously** takes over, it's easy to forget all the neat stuff you do have and how much your parents do for you, too. When this happens, your reacting side may get you to strike out with angry words at a friend, brother, sister, or even a parent.

Before letting this happen, try reading this talk-to-yourself message:

I am feeling so **jealous** right now that I need my thinking side to kick into gear. I know it will help me control these strong feelings of **jealousy**. My thinking side will remind me about what's true, like how my parents really do love me, how I get plenty of stuff, and how it can't always be my turn to get what I want. I can tell my parents that **I'm feeling jealous** and ask for a hug to squeeze those feelings right out of me.

Most times in your life, you expect things to happen the way they happened before. For example, when you go to the movies you expect to get there on time, buy tickets, and enjoy watching the show. But things don't always work out. You might get there late or discover the tickets are sold out. This situation can make you feel very disappointed. Your reacting side may take control, making you feel this is the worst thing in the world. **It can be very hard to be flexible** when you feel this way. **Being flexible** means using your thinking side to handle disappointments so that you can feel better sooner.

Read this talk-to-yourself message to become more flexible:

I must accept that I don't have control over a lot of things in life. I'm going to be disappointed sometimes. I can prepare for this by telling myself to **be flexible**, especially when I'm really looking forward to something. When I do get disappointed, I can tell myself, "Maybe it will work out better for me next time." Even though I can't stop bad things from happening, I can stop myself from reacting so badly to them. **I can be flexible.**

It can be very hard to cooperate when you just don't want to. Your parents (or teachers) may ask you to do something when all you want is for them to leave you alone!

Next time this happens, read this talk-to-yourself message:

Being cooperative is an important part of growing up. Even though it may feel like they're too bossy, my parents and teachers are really trying to help me become more responsible. If I learn how to **be cooperative**, then people will be more likely to **cooperate** with me when I ask them to do stuff. I'll also find that once I simply do what they ask, I'll feel better about myself. Plus, they'll be proud to see that I was able to **cooperate** even when I didn't want to.

Your reacting side makes you feel as if **cooperating** is giving up and caving in. It isn't. **Cooperating** is about letting your thinking side take charge of your behavior. Deep down inside, you know that life goes much more smoothly when you **cooperate**. And remember: **C.T.F.T. (Cooperate the First Time)**. Doing this will lead to the good results that make cooperating worth the effort.

SAY IT AND SHOW IT WHEN YOU GET IT!

BEAT THE FEAR

People probably do nice things for you—buying stuff, driving you places, or just doing you a favor. Problems can occur when you act like you expect nice things from others. You may forget to say **"thank you" and show that you mean it**. Or, you may react like you want something bigger and better. If you do that, people will become angry and you'll end up getting less of what you really want.

Your thinking side can help you remember to say "thank you" and show that you mean it, even if you don't like something all that much.

Read this talk-to-yourself message to learn how:

Sometimes I get what I want and sometimes I get what I don't really want. Either way, somebody is taking the time to do something for me. Even if I don't like something, I should try to remember that the other person wasn't trying to disappoint me. An important part of growing up is **being considerate** of others' feelings. This means saying and **showing that I appreciate the efforts people put into trying to make me happy**.

Fear can creep up on you anytime, anyplace, and about anything. Maybe you **feel scared** as you walk onto the bus, sit in class, or attend some type of practice. **Fear attacks** your body and your mind. Your body feels all wobbly and your thoughts seem to turn against you. You become so worried about something bad happening that you do not deal so well with what is really going on. You end up believing that your **fear** came true—but it didn't. What really happened is that you fell into the **fear trap**.

The next time you start feeling scared, read this talk-to-yourself message:

I am not going to let fear control my reactions anymore. Avoiding things that other kids enjoy **because I'm afraid means less fun for me**. I deserve fun and freedom, too. My thinking side can help me plan ahead to deal with scary things. Things won't always work out the way I want. But when they don't, I'll know **fear** didn't stop me from trying. I am going to use all my courage and determination to **beat the fear** when I feel it creeping up on me.

Being with others sometimes triggers problem behaviors. This can happen at home, school, at a friend's house, around the neighborhood, or just about anywhere. Usually the trigger is something you see or hear, involving the people you're with. Maybe they're upset at someone, are trying to have a private conversation, or have asked you to **butt out**. It can be very hard to do this when you want to be part of what's happening. Maybe you think you have the right solution. Maybe you just want to make yourself feel good or for them to feel bad. You will need to **"back off"** so they can deal with the situation.

Stop yourself from interfering and getting into trouble by reading this talk-to-yourself message:

Knowing when to **back off** will help keep me out of trouble. People don't want me **butting in** when they're trying to deal with something that doesn't involve me. If I interfere, I may become the next target! I can tell myself, "This doesn't involve me and I need to **back off** so that it doesn't become my problem, too." People will like and respect me more when I do this.

A lot goes on in your life every single day. You talk to many different people and spend time in several different places—at home, on the bus, in class, and at friends' houses. While you're at these places and talking with both kids and adults, people notice and listen to you. They notice what you talk about, whether you're listening, and how much you **pay attention to their feelings and ideas**.

You can show people that you are **"tuned in"** by carefully listening to what they say and keeping on the same track when it's your turn to talk. People will like you better when you remember to do this.

Read this talk-to-yourself message as a reminder to stay tuned in:

I will be better at making and keeping friends if I **stay tuned in**. This means not interrupting so much, not assuming others want to hear me talk a lot, and not bringing up something totally different from what's being discussed. **Staying tuned in** means I ask questions, mention things they have told me before, and show my interest by looking right at them.

Like most kids, you probably have lots of energy to do all sorts of things: play sports, go places, enjoy friends, and have fun. When you put that energy into safe activities at the right time, everything goes smoothly. But sometimes your energy comes out at the wrong times—like at school, the dinner table, or family outings. And sometimes your energy even comes out in dangerous ways—like throwing things that shouldn't be thrown, or letting your behavior get out of control. **"Finding the brakes"** means using your thinking side to control your energy.

Read this talk-to-yourself message to learn how to find the brakes:

Having fun, especially with other kids, gives my reacting side a chance to take control. When that happens, fun can quickly turn into trouble, or even danger. At any point, I may need to **find the brakes** and use them to stop my behavior. I keep my **brakes** handy by telling myself that fun doesn't mean I turn my thinking side off. I still need to think about my responsibilities, the rules, and what is safe. I need my thinking side even when I'm having fun.

It's easy to lose track of time while you're having fun. Watching TV, playing video games, using the computer, talking to friends, reading magazines, and stuff like that can become very absorbing. They can **hook** your attention so that important things like homework, chores, or other responsibilities get pushed out of your mind.

Even though it can feel good when you're **"hooked,"** problems develop quickly for kids who let themselves get **hooked.** You can end up in trouble with parents, in school, and even with friends when your time and attention are hooked.

Read this talk-to-yourself message to learn how to watch out for your hooks:

Getting **hooked** means doing so much fun stuff that I let other important things slide. It's okay to have fun, but I need to ask myself, "Am I getting too hooked? Are people telling me that I'm going overboard?" I need to **watch out for my hooks** and realize that they may be fun when I'm doing them, but after I stop, it won't be fun to see the people I've disappointed and to face the work I've let go.

Relationships are like an awesome piece of fabric that offers warmth, protection, and good feelings. But just like pieces of fabric, relationships can **tear** apart because of problems. Too much arguing, not enough cooperating, and saying mean things can leave you and others feeling angry, hurt, and not wanting to be nice. These problems can **tear the fabric** of your relationships with family members, friends, and teachers. If you don't watch out, your reacting side will make things even worse by blaming others for what's going on. Don't let that happen!

Let your thinking side gain control by reading this talk-to-yourself message:

Right now I feel hurt, but that doesn't mean it's all the other person's fault. I had something to do with what happened, even if it was only the way I reacted to what the person did. I can try to **repair the tear** in our relationship by talking softly, saying something nice like, "I'm sorry, I want us to be friends again," and realizing that the other person probably feels hurt, too.

If you lose something like a backpack or a favorite game, you usually try to find it. While the thing is lost, you feel upset and worried. When you find—or recover— whatever you've lost, you feel much better. Things are back in their proper place. What a relief!

You can also lose control over you feelings. When this happens, your reacting side may drum up temper tantrums and crying spells. You may sulk and avoid others. Guess what? You can **recover** control of your feelings just like anything else you lose. When you **recover control over your feelings**, you realize things really aren't so bad after all.

You can learn how to recover more quickly by reading this talk-to-yourself message:

That was upsetting and I still feel kind of shaky. I wish it hadn't happened and that I hadn't lost control of my feelings. But I can't change that now. What I can do is take some deep breaths, count to ten, and recover quickly so my upset feelings won't spread to create more problems. **Quick recovery** brings good feelings back and puts bad feelings behind me, where they belong.

If you're looking forward to doing something you really want to do, you might rush through whatever you don't want to do. Sometimes there are so many things to do that you may feel as if you won't have enough time to do everything. **Rushing** can cause big problems because when you **rush**, you may lose control over your "reacting side." Or, **rushing** through something may mess up how well you do chores, homework, and other stuff like that. When that happens, you usually end up having to do it over again, which ends up taking more time. It can get real frustrating to hear parents and teachers say, "Take your time."

Read this talk-to-yourself message to learn how to slow down:

Rushing through things I don't like doing causes problems. **Slowing down** can actually save me time if I try my hardest to do my best the first time around. I can be much more successful at many more things when I use my thinking side to slow myself down. I do this by telling myself, "Remember, slow down to succeed. I don't always have to race. Doing the very best I can is more important."

All kids hit rough spots. Some hit them more often than others. Rough spots are those times when you're caught off guard by something you didn't **plan**. It could be a test you figured was going to be easy but wasn't, or a promise you made but then forgot about. These situations don't happen because of bad luck. They happen when you don't **plan for what's coming tomorrow, or the next day, or the day after that.** Living for the moment may seem exciting and fun, but rough spots eventually come. If you tend to live in the moment, then you've probably found out that bad things happen to kids who don't **think ahead and prepare.**

Read this talk-to-yourself message to help smooth out your rough spots:

Life goes more smoothly when I **think and plan ahead**. My parents and teachers won't bug me so much and I'll feel better about myself. By remembering to ask myself three questions throughout the day, I can make my life run much more smoothly:

1. **What do I have to remember to do today?**
2. **Before I leave this place, do I have everything I need?**
3. **What's coming up in the next few days that I need to prepare for now?**